# Building Enterprise Taxonomies

## A Controlled Vocabulary Primer

SECOND EDITION

Darin L. Stewart, Ph.D.

Mokita Press

*To Laura,*
*who taught me the importance of details.*

# Contents

# 1

# Findability

"But the plans were on display..."
"On display? I had to go down to the cellar to find them."
"That's the display department."
"With a flashlight."
"Ah, well, the lights had probably gone."
"So had the stairs."
"But look, you found the notice didn't you?"
"Yes," said Arthur, "yes I did. It was on display in the bottom of a locked filing cabinet stuck in a disused lavatory with a sign on the door saying 'Beware of the Leopard.'"

From The Hitchhikers Guide to the Galaxy

Finding good information is hard, much harder than it should be. Your first encounter with a new website often feels like entering a strange land with its own language, laws, customs and culture. You have business to conduct there, but must do so without the benefit of an interpreter or guide. As you begin to explore the homepage, you must quickly orient yourself to its unique approach to navigation, interpret bizarre labels and menus, guess at search terms and wade through propaganda in search of useful information. And these are just the public pages.

Things get much more dangerous if you venture out of the tourist areas and onto an intranet or, heaven help you, a file system. Once you enter the realm of the enterprise information system, all bets are off. The seemingly unified front of the corporate website dissolves into a collection of fiefdoms, each with its own local dialect and jealously guarded borders passable only with the right permissions and passwords. There also seems to be a civil war underway.

Despite our best efforts, most websites, portals, intranets and file systems are hostile environments for information seekers. We hire consultants, hold focus groups and conduct usability studies to understand our users' needs. We build site maps, add search boxes, and tag our content, and users still get lost. According to surveys conducted by Gartner, IDC and others, knowledge workers spend from thirty to as much as forty percent of their work day searching for information and yet only find what they need less than half the time.[1] This means we spend more time looking for documents than actually reading them. This situation is not just embarrassing, it's expensive.

A third of a senior knowledge worker's time, the time they spend chasing information, works out to be roughly $26,000 a year in salary and benefits on average. When those searches are successful, this is a legitimate cost of doing business. When they fail, that fruitless search time is a drain on resources. Yet as expensive as this may seem, search time is a minor component of the cost of hidden information. Even the tens of thousands of dollars spent on redesigning and maintaining an improved website is trivial if it gets users to the content they need. The true cost comes when users throw up their hands and abandon their search. Studies have suggested that this happens after about twelve minutes at the outside.

This phenomenon is not restricted to complex searches and obscure facts. Information as mundane as the contact information for the director of human resources cannot be located by employees on their own Intranet fifty-seven percent of the time. Those intrepid few who can find the information usually must troll through multiple Web pages and documents looking for an org chart (which is probably out of date) that might have the director's name. They must then look up the director in an employee directory located elsewhere on the Intranet hoping they spelled the name right. One study found this to be the case in five out of six corporate Intranets.[2]

When people can't find what they need, they don't just give up. They go elsewhere. When a consumer doesn't find the right product, they go to a competitor, which in aggregate costs your company half of its potential sales. If they are already a customer, they pick up the phone. This costs you an average of seventeen dollars for each call that your self-service website was supposed to eliminate.[3] When an employee can't find what they need, they go to a co-worker, doubling costs while halving productivity and often yielding no better results. In a 2002 research note, Regina Casonato and Kathy Harris of Gartner estimated that an employee will get fifty to seventy-five percent of the information they need directly from other people, effectively erasing the benefits of a corporate Intranet.[4]

When a knowledge worker reaches this dead-end, they have little choice but to set about creating the information they need from scratch. This may be as simple as running a report and stitching a few documents together, but more often it involves considerable research, an additional information chase and consultation with multiple colleagues. Unfortunately, all this effort is not being expended to create information, but to recreate it. As much as ninety percent of the time spent creating information for a specific need is actually recreating information that already exists but could not be located.[5] According to Kit Sims Taylor, this is because it is simply too hard to find what you need.

> At present it is easier to write that contract clause, exam question, insurance policy clause, etc., ourselves than to find something close enough to what we want from elsewhere. ... While most of us do not like to admit that much of our creative work involves reinventing the wheel, an honest assessment of our work would indicate that we do far more 'recreating' than creating.[6]

Taylor has found that in addition to the amount of time spent looking for information, an additional thirty percent is spent reinventing the wheel. When you account for communication and collaboration overhead, only ten percent of our time, effort and energies is actually spent in the creation of new knowledge and information. In a separate study, IDC found that this "knowledge work deficit" costs Fortune 500 companies over twelve billion dollars annually.[7]

These are just the purely quantifiable costs. Consider the impact poor findability has on decision making when there simply isn't time to re-research and recreate the needed intelligence. Critical decisions may be delayed because the information we can find, if any, is either incomplete or conflicting. Worse, bad decisions may be enacted when they wouldn't have even been considered had a fuller, more accurate picture been available. In this age of compliance, the ability to locate and produce information on demand can mean the difference between passing an audit and dissolving the company.

## *Infoglut*

So how did we get into this mess? We have spent literally trillions of dollars on information technology, and yet our access to information seems to get worse in direct proportion to the amount of money and effort expended to improve it. Some pundits point to the sheer volume of information with which we are inundated and resign themselves to this inevitable consequence of life in the information age. As Britton Hadden of *TIME* magazine put it:

> Everyday living is too fast, too busy, too complicated. More than at any other time in history, it's important to have good information on just about every aspect of life. And there is more information available than ever before. Too much in fact. There is simply no time for people to gather and absorb the information they need.

Hadden made this observation in 1929, shortly before founding the magazine. Infoglut is not a new problem, but until recently it was at least somewhat manageable. Today we are discovering that the only thing worse and more dangerous than trying to run an organization with too little information is trying to manage one with too much. Everyone understands intuitively that infoglut is a problem, but few have a clear sense of how much of a problem it really is. Experts have long proclaimed the dangers of information overload. While hyperbole is the lifeblood of consultants, in this case they seem to be right on the money.

Each year the world produces roughly five exabytes ($10^{18}$ *bytes)* of new information. To put that in more familiar terms, if the seventeen million books in the Library of Congress were fully digitized, five exabytes would be the equivalent of 37,000 new libraries each year. While this is staggering in and of itself, consider that in 1999 it is estimated that only two exabytes of new information was created, meaning that the rate of information growth is accelerating by 30% a year. 92% of that information is stored on digital media and 40% is generated by the United States alone. We create 1,397 terabytes of office documents each year. Each day we send thirty-one billion emails.[8] It is no wonder that we are, as John Naisbitt famously put it, "drowning in information, but starved for knowledge."

The deluge has not caught us by surprise. On the contrary, we have attacked it with a vengeance, pouring billions into data warehouses, CRM, ERP, business intelligence and other data management and reporting systems. These efforts and investments have bought us great insight into our *structured content*: that highly organized information structured according to a well defined schema or framework. These are the records found in relational databases and that slot so nicely into spreadsheets and reports. The information contained in these records can easily be located, manipulated and retrieved by means of standard query languages such as SQL.

Unfortunately, this type of domesticated data makes up only fifteen percent of the total information with which we must cope.[9] The remaining eighty-five percent is made up of Web pages, emails, memos, PowerPoint presentations, invoices, product literature, procedure manuals, take-out menus and anything else that doesn't fit neatly into a row in a database. The common factor among all of these different forms of *unstructured content* is that they are all designed for human consumption rather than machine processing. As a result, all of the tried and true methods of data management we have worked so hard to master fail miserably when asked to bring a company picnic announcement to heel. So while quarterly sales forecasts across four continents may be readily available, knowing whether you are supposed to bring a salad or a dessert may be out of reach.

# The Problem with Search

This aspect of the information onslaught has in fact taken us by surprise. Many of us are still in denial. After all, with fully indexed, electronic information sources, full-text searching should allow us to specify all the terms and subjects in which we are interested and have the information retrieved and delivered to our desktop. As any user of Google, A9, or countless other search and retrieval engines has learned through painful experience, things rarely work out that neatly.

Rather than receiving a nice, neat set of targeted documents, search engines generally present us with long lists of Web pages that merely contain the words on which we searched. Whether or not those words are used in the manner and context we intended (did you mean Mercury the planet, the car, the Roman God or the element?) isn't part of the equation. We are left to sort through page after page of links looking for something that might be relevant.

Part of this problem is self-inflicted. People just don't write good queries. One third of the time, search engine users only specify a single word as their query and on average use only two or three.[10] This is what leads to so many irrelevant documents being returned. We don't give enough context to our subject to eliminate documents that are not of interest. If you query just on the term "Washington" you will receive links to information on the state, the president, the capital, a type of apple, a movie star, a university and so forth. In all, Google returns 1,180,000,000 "hits." If you add the term "Denzel" the number of links drops to 3,520,000, and we are reasonably focused on the actor. If we add the phrase "Academy Award" we finally get to 107,000 documents reasonably focused on the actor's accolades. So the more specific and verbose we are with our queries the more relevant the results.

But what happens if you use the Academy Award's common nickname "Oscar" in your query? The number of hits jumps to 593,000. This is the risk of getting too specific with search terms. By using the proper name of the award rather than its popular name, we may have missed 486,000 potentially relevant documents. Guessing the wrong search term can have a dramatic impact on what you do and don't find.

Information scientists have long been aware that there are tradeoffs between depth and coverage whenever a search is conducted. The broader the search is, the more documents that are retrieved, including those that are not relevant to the actual information need. Conversely, the deeper or narrower the search, the more likely retrieved documents are to be relevant. The cost, of course, is that it is also more likely that documents of interest will be missed in the search. The difficulty arises from the fine balance of *precision* and *recall*.

**Precision** is usually described as a ratio: the number of *relevant* documents retrieved divided by the total number of documents retrieved. In other words, what percentage of the total number of documents retrieved are actually related to the topic being investigated? For example, a Google search on the terms "precision" and "recall" returns approximately 970,000 documents. The first few documents in the list do indeed prove to be related to measures of search performance. However, a few links into the list a news item appears: "Vermont Precision Woodworks Announce Recall of Cribs." From the search engine's perspective, this is a perfectly valid document. It contains both of the search terms in its title. In fact, one search term appears in the title of the website itself, www.recall-warnings.com, thus causing it to receive a high relevancy ranking. Out of 970,000 documents, it is safe to assume that many, if not most, of the retrieved documents will have this level of relevancy to our query. This indicates low precision, but high recall.

**Recall** is also a ratio and is defined as the number of relevant documents retrievedthe total number of relevant documents in the collection being searched. The example above probably has a high recall due to the large number of documents returned.

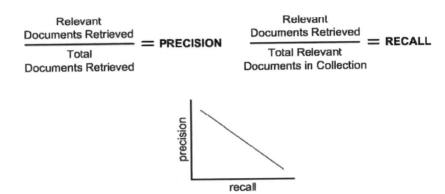

These two measures are inversely related: as recall increases, precision decreases. A balance must be found between the two, retrieving enough documents to get an individual the information they need without returning so many that wading through irrelevant information becomes burdensome. This balance is the heart of information retrieval, but it is difficult to measure precision and recall precisely. This is because we rarely know what is contained in the collection we are searching, in this case the Internet itself, and also because the notion of relevance is very subjective. At best we can estimate recall and precision based on feedback from users of the search engine in question and make adjustments as appropriate.

Taking our Google search on "precision" and "recall" as a test case, it may seem that the problem isn't so bad. After all, the first several documents in the list were on the exact topic we were seeking: search performance measures. We can just disregard the other 3.5 million documents offered. We got what we needed from the top ten or twenty.

This ability to rank pertinent documents near the top of a result set is what has made Google the clear winner of the search engine wars. Their PageRank algorithm is a key ingredient in the Google secret sauce.[11] Rather than just counting how many times a certain word occurs in a document or where it occurs, Google also looks at who links to that document. If a lot of pages reference a particular website, chances are that it is a pretty important source of information on the topic at hand. If the pages linking in are themselves important, then that likelihood increases and the document's relevancy rank improves accordingly. This variation on "citation analysis," which is traditionally used to determine the importance of scholarly publications, has radically changed Internet search for the better. Google even offers a free tool that I can add to my website to search my own content with just a few lines of code.

So, problem solved? Not quite. There are several caveats to applying a Google-like tool to your findability challenges. First, Google free site search is really only searching a subset of the entire Google index, that part representing just your website. As a result, only those Web pages that are open and available to the public will be included in a search. Anything on the Intranet is invisible to the Google spiders, the programs that find and index Web pages and build up the search index. Even those pages and documents that are open to the Internet at large may be missed. Indexing programs only go so deep when looking over a website. If your content is more than a link or two away from the main page, it will probably be missed. Any new content you add will likewise be invisible until the next time an indexing spider happens by—a process completely outside of your control. As Google explains:

> There are a number of reasons a page might not appear in the results of your Google free site search. It could be that Google hasn't crawled that particular page yet. Google refreshes its index frequently, but some pages are inevitably missed. Or, the page may have Javascript, frames, or store information in a database. Pages like these are difficult or impossible for the Google crawler to visit and index.[12]

Finally, Google's greatest strength, the PageRank algorithm, is also its greatest weakness when applied to a single website. It is unlikely that CNN.com or eBay will reference your org chart. In fact, very few websites outside of your organization will link to your internal documents. Yet the rankings applied to your documents are determined in the context of rankings of the Internet as a whole. This effectively renders the relevancy judgments made on your content meaningless when the search is restricted to your own site.[13]

Aside from the arcane nature of indexing, the very act of searching can be a struggle in most organizations. Documents and content are spread out across multiple locations and repositories. Policies may be on the Intranet, quarterly reports on the file system, resumes in a departmental directory and price lists on the company homepage. Finding information is no longer an exercise in finding a needle in a haystack. First you must choose which haystacks to search, in what order, and for how long. In most organizations, less than half of their documents are centrally indexed.[14] This means that it is impossible to look for information in all potential locations with a single query or even a single search tool. This dispersal of information across an organization leads to another search challenge: choosing the correct query terms.

```
<!-- SiteSearch Google -->
<FORM method=GET action="http://www.google.com/search">
<input type=hidden name=ie value=UTF-8>
<input type=hidden name=oe value=UTF-8>
<TABLE bgcolor="#FFFFFF"><tr><td>
<A HREF="http://www.google.com/">
<IMG SRC="http://www.google.com/logos/Logo_40wht.gif"
border="0" ALT="Google"></A>
</td><td>
<INPUT TYPE=text name=q size=31 maxlength=255 value="">
<INPUT type=submit name=btnG VALUE="Google Search">
<font size=-1>
<input type=hidden name=domains value="YOUR DOMAIN NAME"><br>
<input type=radio name=sitesearch value=""> WWW <input type=radio
name=sitesearch value="YOUR DOMAIN NAME" checked> YOUR DOMAIN NAME
<br></font></td></tr></TABLE>
</FORM>
<!-- SiteSearch Google -->
```

**Figure 2.  Just cut, paste and you've got search.  Not quite.**

Most search engines create their indexes by extracting terms from the full text of documents. As a result content creators and authors become de facto indexers and catalogers. The words they choose in authoring their documents become the search terms available to their readers. This becomes a problem if they don't speak the same language. This goes back to the Mercury (planet, car, god) and actor (Academy Award or Oscar) problem.

**Figure 3. The ideal relationship between author and searcher.**

Unless there is a company standard for terminology, and these are rare, each area of an enterprise is going to have its own language. A *customer* in one area may be a *client* in another and a *patron* somewhere else. This lack of consistency in search and indexing terms has proven to be the single greatest challenge to the effectiveness of search and findability in general.[15]

Ultimately, any search consists of, at minimum, four hurdles that must be cleared. First, the information seeker must be able to articulate what they are looking for with the right syntax for the specific search tool being used. Next, they must guess what words an author may have used to express the concept of interest. Then, with the query in mind, they must figure out the most likely place to search. Finally, they must sift through the results of their search, separating the potentially relevant from the clearly irrelevant and hope what they end up with is complete, representing all that is available. Really, it's a wonder that we ever find anything at all.

# *Teleporting and Orienteering*

A keyword search is most often an attempt (usually several attempts, actually) to go directly and instantaneously to the exact location of desired information. If we search the Web on the terms "Aladdin Theater Box-Office" we hope to land where we can purchase tickets for concerts at this small venue in Portland, Oregon, without having to sift through irrelevant information. The academic community has labeled this sort of information seeking behavior **teleporting**.[16]

Teleporting is one **strategy** for finding information and can be executed in various ways with a number of search **tactics**. In addition to keyword search, an information seeker may attempt to teleport by specifying a specific URL, opening a certain email, or typing in a directory path to a particular document. Perfect teleporting (hitting your target on the first attempt) is a rare accomplishment; so rare in fact that a game, "Google Whacking," has sprung up around the challenge.[17] Yet despite the difficulty in finding just the right information with search alone, most websites and information portals seem designed to encourage the attempt as evidenced by the ubiquitous search box.

A more realistic scenario is to teleport into the general vicinity of the information you are seeking, using search or some other tactic, and then zero in on your target with a succession of small steps. To buy our concert tickets for a show at the Aladdin, for example, we might teleport by typing in the URL for the theater: www.aladdin-theater.com. We know we are close, but still can't buy our tickets so we may follow the link to the "Upcoming Shows" page. Here we find the performer we are looking for listed with a link to "show details" so we click through to that page. Finally we see a banner for "Local Ticket Outlet Information," which leads us to a link for the "Aladdin Theater Online Ticketing Page" where we can order our tickets.

This strategy of locating information by continually narrowing our search through incremental steps has been dubbed **orienteering** (though most people simply call it browsing) and has proven to be the preferred approach to finding information. Studies conducted at the MIT Artificial Intelligence lab have found that information seekers use keyword search less than forty percent of the time. Surprisingly, this holds true even when searchers know exactly what they are looking for and even where to find it (see table 1). [18]

| | Specific Information | General Information | Specific Document | Total |
|---|---|---|---|---|
| Orienteering | 47 | 19 | 41 | 120 |
| Teleporting | 34 | 23 | 17 | 80 |
| Total | 81 | 42 | 58 | 200 |

**Table 1. Information need by search strategy** (19 unknowns removed).

There are circumstances where keyword search yields nominally better results than navigation. In one study, information seekers were more successful at locating information on a well indexed medical information site by using search rather than browsing. Interestingly, those most successful at finding what they were looking for were those individuals who turned to search only after browsing failed (see figure 3). Even when individuals abandon browse on a given information hunt and succeed with search, they invariably return to orienteering on their next task. [19]

M.I.T. researchers have found several reasons why people prefer to zero in on information rather than attempting to pounce on it in a single great leap. First, it can be difficult to clearly articulate exactly what it is you are seeking. This is the case even when trying to retrieve familiar information and documents. Think of the last time you were asked for directions to a familiar destination. Even though you may be able to drive there without thinking, you may have a hard time giving step by step instructions on how to get to that same location. Browsing reduces the cognitive demand on information seekers by allowing them to follow familiar paths to the general area of the information they are seeking, quickly and easily reducing the size of the area they must explore. This also allows searchers to draw

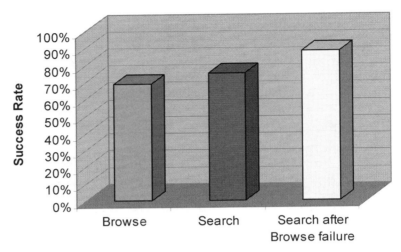

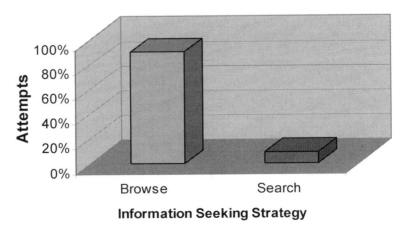

Figure 4. Information seeking behaviors.

on a broad range of "meta-information" about the target of their search.

For example, say you need to locate a company memo that was circulated six months ago and has since disappeared into the bowels of the company Intranet. Even though you have no idea where to find the memo itself, you recall seeing it referred to in an email from a colleague. You may not know exactly where to find that email either, but you likely will recall who it was from and roughly when you received it, along with some idea of the subject line and general content. This will allow you to find the email that will in turn point you toward the actual target of your search—the company memo. Even though you can't teleport even into the general vicinity of the memo, you can start from a known frame of reference (the email) and follow clues along the way until you arrive at your goal.

The small steps of orienteering and the clues found along the way also provide information seekers with a strong sense of location throughout their search. The importance of the "you are here" factor should not be underestimated. When users feel in control and that they are heading in the right direction and are able to backtrack if they take a wrong turn, they are less likely to abandon a search prematurely. When people drop into the middle of an information space as a result of a keyword search, they have no context and little indication of how to proceed. This sense of disorientation can cause both knowledge workers and potential customers to leave a website as quickly as they arrive.

By contrast, navigating through an information space allows the user to become acclimated to the environment at their own pace, much like easing into a hot bath rather than plunging into scalding water. This process of guided exploration also has the dual benefit of building context for interpreting the target information once it is found and allowing for serendipitous discoveries along the way. Most importantly, information seekers are more likely to continue their search if they are confident that they are on the right path and that their efforts will pay off.

**Figure 5.  Breadcrumb trails are often used to give users a sense of control over their exploration of a new information space.**

It's interesting to note that the word **browse** derives from an antiquated French term *brost* meaning "young shoot" and referring to the way that animals feed on the young shoots of trees and shrubs. As animals seek for nourishment, they must balance the nutrition to be gained against the energy expended obtaining it. This behavior is fundamentally the same for information seekers. Visitors to an information space, whether it be a website, Intranet, database, file system or what have you, are continually balancing cost and benefit: "Will the information I find here be worth the time and effort it is costing me to track it down?" As they browse a website, they will be repeatedly assessing the likelihood of finding what they need in the current environment and determining when it's time to move on to more promising pastures.

This metaphor has become the basis of **information foraging theory**, a model of information-seeking behavior developed by Peter Pirolli and Stuart Card of the Xerox Palo Alto Research Center.[20] According to this model, we search for information across the Internet using essentially the same strategies hunter-gatherers use to search for food across the savannah. The nature of the prey may be new, but the fundamental approach hasn't changed for millennia. Both animals and humans attempt to maximize their "benefit per unit cost." When the **benefit**, in terms of likelihood of finding the necessary food or information with an acceptable investment of time and energy, falls below a certain threshold, the current website or watering hole will be labeled sterile and the forager moves on to a more fertile **patch**. Steps can be taken to reduce the likelihood of users leaving our information patches prematurely. One of the most effective strategies is to increase the strength of the information scent present in our systems.

The notion of **information scent** is central to information foraging. The basic idea is that just like a game animal, information leaves behind **spoor** that can be detected and tracked.

> Associated concepts "rub off" on one another, leaving detectable traces, just as a watering hole frequented by woolly mammoths will smell of woolly mammoths. A hunter-gatherer seeking mammoths is likely to be drawn to the watering hole, if only to look for spoor. Information foragers do the same. Imagine you're looking for texts about foraging theory. If [a search] throws up a box containing the keyword "hunter-gatherer", you're likely to select that box. It just smells right. [21]

Consider our ticket purchasing example. When we first arrive at the theater's homepage, we see labels such as "Artist of the Month" and "Show Listings," which may even include the concert we are seeking. Even though we don't see that we can purchase tickets here, the page smells like concert tickets so we continue our search by clicking on "Upcoming Shows." Here the scent gets stronger when we find the right show along with a link to "Show Details," which finally gets us to "Buy Tickets Online." Throughout the process of browsing, the scent of concert tickets is strong and gets stronger the closer we get to our goal. This continual positive feedback can keep information seekers happy with the current information patch and prevent them from jumping to a competitor or colleague to meet their needs.

Strong information scent can be a double-edged sword if mishandled. The most common pitfall occurs when a strong scent points toward what should be the right answer but isn't. Jakob Nielsen demonstrated this phenomenon in a study of a health information for teens website. [22] Users were asked to find out how much they could weigh without being considered overweight. Most users quickly gravitated toward an area of the site labeled "Food & Fitness." This clear, concise label had strong information scent for the question at hand. Featured prominently within that area of the site was a lengthy article entitled "What's the right weight for my height?" that was also ranked highly by a search on the term "weight."

This would seem to be a bull's-eye except for the fact that the article does not contain the answer to the question. Because the information scent leading to this article was so strong, users were convinced they were looking in the right place. When the information wasn't there, they naturally concluded that because it wasn't where it should be, it must not exist anywhere on the site and abandoned their search. This is an unfortunate result since the answer was in fact available on the site. It was buried in an article titled "Body Mass Index (BMI)." The information scent of this title for answering the target question is almost non-existent. First, the title is a bit academic and maybe even intimidating for the website's teenage audience. Worse, the title gives no indication of the article's content which includes a straightforward

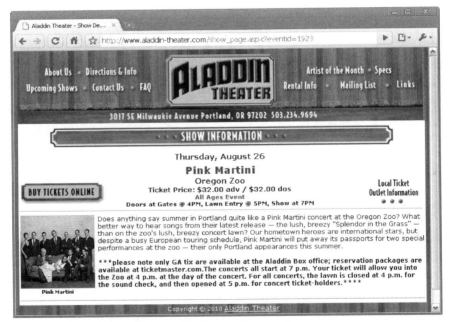

**Figure 6. A website with good information scent.**

calculation of optimal weight using height, weight and age. In a nutshell, the container of the information was mislabeled.

The problem of bad labels strikes at the heart of findability. If information seekers cannot recognize the content they are searching for even when they find it, it may as well not exist. Even when an information producer gives careful consideration to labeling and categorization, the result may have no meaning to information consumers. A physician, wanting to be precise, may label a document on treating a particular respiratory condition with the terms laryngotracheobronchitis, inspiratory stridor and dexamethasone. While this may be perfectly appropriate for other doctors, it is of little use to a mother searching the Web for information on how to alleviate the wheezing cough of her daughter with croup.

Most information systems today are organized much like libraries before Melvil Dewey created his decimal system for classification. Patrons were left to wander stacks of untitled or oddly titled books piled on shelves according to some idiosyncratic organizational scheme comprehended only by an arcane priesthood of local librarians.

Overcoming this barrier to discovery is the role of controlled vocabularies and taxonomies. By developing a structured collection of terms and guidelines around how they are to be applied, information can be managed in a manner that facilitates its discovery, interpretation and use to the greatest extent possible.

Beyond just finding information, the hierarchical nature of a taxonomy can help educate an information seeker by guiding them through a subject. The mother searching for information about her daughter's illness will not only discover that dexamethasone is a steroidal treatment for the condition, but that humidified air may also alleviate her discomfort. Continuing through the structure she will discover additional treatments and potential complications. Finally, she will learn that the proper name for "croup" is in fact *laryngotracheobronchitis*, giving her a new term to search on and expanding the potential information sources available to her.

The **parent/child relationships** inherent in the **tree** structure of a taxonomy are powerful tools in guiding a seeker through what may be an unfamiliar subject. By explicitly showing how terms and concepts are related, a searcher will discover associations that they didn't know existed. Most importantly, they can define and refine their information need as they explore rather than having to precisely articulate it up front when they may not know exactly what it is they are seeking.

Organizing information according to a well defined structure, such as a taxonomy, also provides stability to an information environment. Information changes continually. Delphi Group has estimated that at least ten percent of enterprise information changes monthly in an average organization.[23] Without some means of governance, relevant information becomes a moving target. Today a search on "taxonomies" may yield 1,900,000 matches. Tomorrow or next week that same query could return 1,985,000 hits with completely different rankings. That article I found last week that was so useful but that I didn't bookmark could now be anywhere.

A taxonomy can act as a dynamic bookmark. As new documents and information become available, they can be classified, labeled and published in accordance with the taxonomy without changing its structure. When a knowledge worker needs to return to an area of interest, he will still find it where he left it. The only difference will be that there is now more information available there. In addition, the new information will be in context with relationships and potential avenues of exploration clearly visible.

Managing terms and keywords can also enhance search by bridging the vocabulary gap between information producer and consumer. A search engine integrated with a taxonomy would know that a search on *croup* should also look for *laryngotracheobronchitis* and that in certain contexts "Oscar" is another way of saying "Academy Award." It can also compensate for common spelling errors and variants (i.e., theatre or theater) and synonyms (fall or plunge or spill or tumble). These expansions may seem trivial, but they can dramatically improve the effectiveness and efficiency of search.

## A sample hierarchy of respiratory illnesses

**CROUP**
(USE FOR laryngotracheobronchitis)
**Symptoms**
       fever
       wheezing
       (USE FOR inspiratory stridor)
       swollen lymph glands
       decreased appetite
**Treatment**
       humidified air
       fever reducer
          acetaminophen
          ibuprofen
       steroid
          dexamethasone
          prelone
          orapred
          pulmicort
       breathing treatment
          acemic epinephrine
**Complication**
       kidney inflammation
       (USE FOR glomerulonephritis)
       rheumatic fever


**STREP THROAT**
**Symptoms**
       fever
       swollen lymph glands
       rash
**Treatment**
       antibiotic
          amoxicillin
          erythromycin
**Complication**
       rheumatic fever


**RESPIRATORY SYNCYTIAL VIRUS**
(USE RSV)
**Symptoms**
       ...

Controlled vocabularies, like taxonomy and its relatives, are not silver bullets and will not magically cure all information management problems, but they are a critical component of findability. If properly constructed, applied and maintained, a taxonomy can radically increase the value of information by making it more available, understandable and actionable. The remainder of this book will demonstrate how this can be achieved. Before we can delve into the mysteries and wonders of taxonomies, however, we must take a brief detour into the world of **metadata**.

# 2

# Metadata

If we fail to anticipate the unforeseen or expect the unexpected in a universe of infinite possibilities, we may find ourselves at the mercy of anyone or anything that cannot be programmed, categorized or easily referenced.

Fox Mulder, "The X-Files"

Art collecting is a tricky business. The value of a painting, sculpture or even a rare book can vary wildly depending on the circumstances of a purchase. Two similar works by Monet may go on the auction block together; one sells for thousands, the other for millions. The only substantive difference between the two is the existence of provenance information. A clear record of a painting's history, who has owned it, when and where it has previously sold and for how much is essential to determining whether or not it is a wise investment. Without such information we have no context for our decision. Is it overpriced or undervalued? Is it stolen? Is it a verified Monet or just a suspected Monet? Even though it is the painting itself that holds our interest, we need information *about* the painting to qualify our interest. This same principle applies to less tangible assets—namely information.

When we first locate new information we tend to be suspicious. Can I trust these numbers? Is this the current version of the document? Is this image copyright cleared? This is especially true if the source of that information is not familiar to us. Before we trust a document or a Web page, we need to know a little more about it. Some of these questions may be answered by the search itself. When we look for information, we usually try to specify parameters to limit the scope of the search. Specifying the author of a document, the date of its publication, whether it is a report, invoice, form or memo will not only enhance our chances of locating what we are looking for but can pre-qualify the content as it is found. This kind of reference information is generally not indicated explicitly in the content itself, but rather is supplementary to it. It is **metadata**.

The standard definition of metadata is usually given as "data about data." This gets at the general idea, but is not quite adequate. The term "meta" comes from the Greek root meaning *something that follows another and takes it into account*. Thus, metadata is generally developed from associated source data and as a function of the information it describes. The Greek term also means *among, alongside,* or *with*, so it follows that metadata can take several complementary forms in relationship to its parent information. Finally, if the Latin derivation is taken into account, meta can mean *transcendent*, so metadata should be expected to add value above and beyond the content it describes.

To complicate matters, the distinction between data and metadata can be fluid. What is metadata in one context may be pure data in another. For example, if you are looking for an article on a certain topic by a certain author, then the writer's name and the subject keywords are metadata and the content of the article is data. By contrast, say you are trying to remember the name of the author who wrote a particular article in the 1940s and can't remember the title. You do remember that it contained the phrase: "Man cannot hope fully to duplicate this mental process artificially, but he certainly ought to be able to learn from it." In this case the publication date range, 1940–1949, and the content of the article itself are the metadata and the author's name is the data.[1]

# *The Value of Metadata*

In late 1988, a non-descript van pulled up in front of Christie's East, the purchasing office of the renowned auction house in New York City. Tied to its top with several lengths of rope was a six by seven foot canvas. The driver had found it at a warehouse sale of unclaimed property and purchased it on a whim for $1,000. The painting was in bad shape and nothing was known about it, but it was large and old and ought to be worth something. He offered it to Christie's for $1,500. Ian Kennedy, a resident expert of Old Masters for Christie's examined the painting an instantly recognized it as a work of the Italian Master Dosso Dossi. With this new bit of information, the asking price rose from $1,500 to $800,000. It was purchased by the London art dealers Hazlitt, Gooden & Fox for $4 million, dirt, rips and all. Two months later it was sold to the Getty Museum for an even higher price.

**"Allegory of Fortune," Dosso Dossi**

The defining characteristic of metadata is that whatever form it takes, it facilitates the identification and discovery of a discrete package of information. The classic example of this is the library catalog card. Independent of any actual content from the item being described, a simple 3" x 5" card can provide a wealth of information that is useful in locating and managing an information resource, in this case a book. At a glance, we can determine the title, author, publisher, length, topic and even location of the book. This quick access is by design.

```
973.4
B21     McCullough, David G.
        John Adams / [by] David McCullough
        New York : Simon & Schuster, c2001
        751 p., [40] p. of plates : ill. (some col.),
              maps ; 25 cm.

        Includes bibliographical references (p. 703-726)
                and index.
            ISBN 0-7432-2313-6

        1. Adams, John, 1735-1826,   2. Presidents - United
        States - Biography.    3. United States - Politics
        and government - 1783-1809.   I. Title.

                    E.322.M38    2001
                    973.4'4'092 [B]   2001027010
```

**Figure 1. Metadata in a traditional card catalog.**

An often overlooked feature of the humble card catalog is that the cards are organized to facilitate this at-a-glance utility. Each card has a consistent location and format for each piece of information it contains. When looking at an author card, we know the first line indicates the author of the work and the second line is the book's title. The structure of the card tells us that a book is a biography of John Adams written by David McCullough rather than the other way around. The same principle applies to electronic resources. To be useful, metadata must be structured to facilitate both discovery and interpretation.

Most major newspapers now provide online editions with searchable full-text archives. If we type in a few well chosen key words, we have a chance of finding something of interest. The newspaper's search engine will match our query terms against every word of every article of every edition contained in the archive. This is searching the *data*, the actual content of the newspapers. This type of search is subject to all of the pitfalls of unconstrained search as discussed in the prior chapter. If we instead search the *metadata*, we can dramatically improve the effectiveness of our search.

**Figure 2. The advanced search page of the LA Times.**

If we would like to research the position of former president Jimmy Carter on U.S. trade with China, a reasonable place to start is the archives of the *Los Angeles Times* (www.latimes.com). As we would expect, searching on the keywords "Carter," "Policy," and "China" returns an assortment of documents ranging from an analysis of the conflict between China and Taiwan to an obituary of Stanford University professor Michael Oksenberg. Fortunately, the *Times* archive provides an advanced search mechanism utilizing extensive metadata. Rather than a blind search where all words are treated equally, the *Times* enables users to restrict certain terms to certain areas. We can specify that "Jimmy Carter" only be matched against authors and that only articles of the type "opinion piece" with the word "China" in the headline be retrieved. Even though we are no longer looking at any of the archive's actual data or article text and are instead searching only metadata, we receive a precise set of documents with a strong likelihood of being relevant to our interest.

# Types of Metadata

The advantages metadata affords to searching electronic versions of traditional textual resources are straightforward. However, the digital world isn't as simple a place as it once was, and newspapers, magazine articles and the like are rapidly becoming a minority among the milieu of online information. New types of information objects and artifacts seem to emerge daily. In order to manage this deluge of new forms of information, we must be able to describe them in ways that are specific to each unique type and the tasks utilizing them. To this end, several different forms of metadata—descriptive, technical, and administrative—may be developed for any given information object.

# Descriptive Metadata

**Descriptive metadata** is by far the most common form of metadata in use today and is usually what you will encounter as an information seeker. This type of metadata comprises what is explicitly added to content to make it easier to find. In a nutshell, descriptive metadata is the who, what, when, and where of an information resource. While it found its first broad application with textual resources such as the *LA Times* archives, it is rapidly coming to permeate every aspect of the online world.

Take for example, Apple Computer's popular iTunes online music service. Since the content offered by iTunes is non-textual (i.e., the strains of a Bach concerto or a John Coltrane solo), full-text search of the content itself is ill-suited to retrieval. Rather, you search the textual information associated with the audio or video file you are trying to find. Most files have been extensively **tagged** with descriptive metadata. This includes the basics, such as artist, album, and song title as well as more advanced categories such as genre, sub-genre, release date and publisher. Each piece of metadata associated

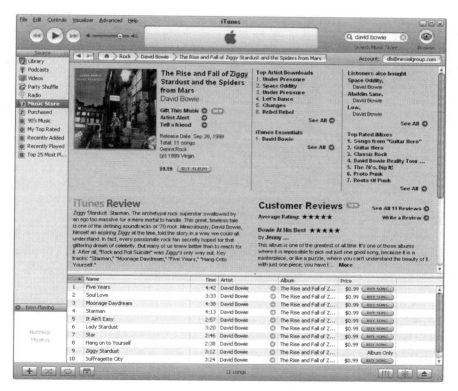

**Figure 3. Metadata in iTunes.**

with a particular song increases the probability that it will be found, either by searching or browsing, and subsequently sold.

The value of descriptive metadata doesn't rest solely in discovery and retrieval. It also facilitates the second part of the e-commerce equation: making the sale. Once a user browses through genres, sub-genres, and artists to a particular album of interest they can read reviews, ratings, song length, and even beats per minute. All of this is descriptive metadata that will help the information seeker make a value judgment of the content they are considering. The principle is equally valid for corporate earnings reports as it is for Mariah Carey videos.

## *Administrative Metadata*

If descriptive metadata is intended primarily for the information seeker, **administrative metadata** is mainly for the benefit of the information owner or **steward**. Metadata elements specifying from where a file or document came, where it is to be hosted, who is authorized to modify it, when it is to be archived, in what form and for how long are all administrative metadata. It is created for the purposes of management, decision making and record keeping.[3]

Administrative metadata is the lifeblood of modern content, document and records management systems. It allows content to move through its lifecycle in a largely automated fashion. For example, companies try to keep their websites interesting by continually changing their content. New stories are posted to the homepage and older content is moved to less prominent locations. A few well chosen pieces of metadata, such as publish date, run length, and archive page ID can combine with business rules in a content management system to automate for the most part the entire process of updating a website. This frees the Web team to focus on creating compelling content rather than shuffling files around the server. It also allows the website to be updated in the middle of the night without disturbing the webmaster's sleep.

Recently, administrative metadata has found a new niche in the form of **Digital Rights Management** (DRM). Once the province of military intelligence and industrial secrets, DRM has recently moved into the mainstream. As distribution of intellectual property across the Internet and corporate Intranets has become the norm, having a reliable means to track that content and control who can access it has become essential. DRM secures digital materials and limits access to only those with the proper authorization. In addition, a complete DRM solution facilitates and tracks any transactions involving the content you wish to protect. For example, allowing copying or limiting the period of access or the number of times content may be viewed must all be supported.[4] DRM technologies and techniques are driven by administrative metadata.

# *Structural Metadata*

As we have noted, information comes in many forms and from many sources, usually bundled into packages that are largely black boxes to us. How are we, or more importantly the tools we use, to know how the information is to be read, manipulated and displayed? How does an application know the technical requirements for integrating the contents of some strange new file into its world so that we may have access to its contents? This is the role of **structural metadata**.

Structural metadata, sometimes referred to as **technical metadata**, **display metadata** or **use metadata**, describes how an information object, usually a file or set of related files, is put together. This can range from technical details such as file size, compression scheme, and scanning resolution to display and navigation information such as presentation order, typographic instructions, and search mechanisms.

The most common application of structural metadata is defining how information is to be organized in databases and data warehouses. Every piece of information housed in a database must be grouped into records and described in terms of type, size, and relationships.

The structural metadata governing this organization is in fact what makes up a database and turns unorganized data into a usable collection of structured information.

Another way of looking at structural metadata is the **page-turner model**. In this model, structural metadata specifies how individual information objects are bound together to make up a single information package that is presented in a specific order, like the pages and chapters of a book. This allows text, images, and other content to be presented in sequence, but enables the user to navigate it at will, jumping from section to section, while preserving the organization and structure originally intended by the creator.


## *Metadata Schemas*

Regardless of its type—descriptive, administrative or structural—and the purpose to which it is applied, all metadata share certain characteristics. At a minimum metadata must posses semantics, syntax, and structure.[5]

**Semantics** refers to the meaning of metadata *within a particular community* or **domain**. It is important to note that any given metadata field can have different interpretations depending on the context in which it is being used. For example, the administrative field *sample source* could refer to a medical procedure or even a particular patient in a medical context, or it could refer to a certain musical instrument or recording in the context of audio production. It could just as easily be a technical field referencing a particular device or encoding scheme. The point is that without clearly defined semantics, it is nearly impossible to accurately interpret metadata.

Just as people cannot interpret metadata without an understanding of its semantics, computers can't make sense of it without syntax and structure. **Syntax** is the systematic arrangement of metadata elements and their values according to well defined rules. The most common form of syntax currently is the name-value pair in which the name of the metadata element is simply matched with its value, such as:

```
<author = Arturo Perez-Reverte>
<title = The Club Dumas>
<genre = Fiction>
```

**Structure** defines how metadata is to be organized to ensure consistent representation and interpretation in line with its syntax and semantics. The structure specifies which metadata elements are allowed where, in what order and how often. A record describing a "book" must start with one or more authors, followed by a single title, a single genre, an optional sub-genre, a single publisher and so forth.

Taken together, semantics, syntax, and structure form a type of grammar, called a **schema**, that specifies the rules governing the metadata of any given domain or application. At the most basic level, a schema specifies a list of attributes that are valid for describing an information package. A more sophisticated schema will often detail out every aspect of how metadata is to be encoded and represented. In all cases the overarching goal of defining a rich schema is to make metadata as useful as possible in terms of interoperability, extensibility and flexibility.

**Interoperability** is the ability of information systems to exchange metadata and interact in a useful way over communication networks such as the Internet.[6] This is what allows the computers at Amazon.com to talk to your bank or credit card company and receive payment for the book you ordered. **Extensibility** means that the original definition of the schema isn't the final word. It should always be possible to add additional metadata elements (albeit in an organized and controlled manner) to any schema in order to accommodate specific and often unforeseen user needs.

Above all, metadata users demand **flexibility** from their metadata schemes and systems. They do not want to be compelled to add information that they deem is irrelevant or too cumbersome. As a result, most metadata schemas allow authors to include as much or as little detail as they desire in a metadata record. This makes authors happy, but tends to make life difficult for information and metadata administrators, since the more flexible metadata is, the less interoperable it becomes. Two information systems may depend on a particular metadata element in order to communicate, and if an author fails to provide it, interaction between the two systems becomes impossible. Imagine if Amazon.com neglected to include the price of a book when it tried to charge your credit card. Schemas serve to mitigate these problems while preserving as much flexibility as possible.

The number of publicly available schemas has exploded in recent years, and there now seems to be metadata standards (official, de facto, and even competing) for nearly every domain imaginable. One of the earliest and most broadly applied is the **Dublin Core** (DC). Named after the Ohio city in which it was first drafted, the Dublin Core was originally developed with an eye to describing document-like objects. More recently, DC metadata is beginning to be applied to a broad range of other types of resources as well.

One of the strengths of DC and a prime reason for its popularity is its simplicity. The DC schema captures the fundamental characteristic of an information resource in a manner that is easy to create and comprehend. Thomas Baker of the German National Research Center for Information Technology has referred to it as "metadata pidgin for digital tourists."[7]

In its current form, DC consists of fifteen elements covering the basic descriptive, administrative and structural needs of an information object. For each element the schema supplies both an official **label** and a concise definition. For example *creator* is defined as: "an entity primarily responsible for making the content of the resource." Just as with a well defined structure, clear definitions of labels and terms are essential to ensuring the appropriate interpretation and application of metadata.

The Dublin Core is an example of a simple schema that can mediate between the extremes of full indexing of raw text and highly structured content. It provides a mechanism for capturing the fundamental information necessary to describe an information resource without the burden of elements that may be irrelevant to a particular community or application.

Some have perceived the spare nature of DC schema as a weakness. While its basic nature allows it to describe many different types of resources, it limits the detail you can capture about that resource. For example, the **creator** element, described above, makes no distinction between a person, an organization, or a service. This could be essential information to a particular application. Perhaps even more troublesome is the fact that there are no constraints placed on the **values** a given element may take. For example, the **subject** element can be filled with a keyword, a Library of Congress Subject Heading or a free text description. This lack of standard terms and values is critical, as we shall see shortly.

| Descriptive | Administrative | Structural |
| --- | --- | --- |
| Title | Creator | Date |
| Subject | Publisher | Type |
| Description | Contributor | Format |
| Source | Rights | Identifier |
| Language | | |
| Relation | | |
| Coverage | | |

**Figure 4. The current Dublin Core element set.**

These shortcomings are common to most metadata schemas. The Dublin Core is a good example of how limitations can be overcome through extensibility. The DC supports two types of qualifiers, **schemes** and **types**, which refine the base schema.

Schemas allow you to specify the standard syntax or vocabulary that are allowable for element values. The DC element *subject* may be qualified with **MESH** to indicate that all values must be drawn from the Medical Subject Headings vocabulary or **LCSH** to require Library of Congress terms. Likewise the language element may be qualified with **ISO 639-2RFC 3066** to ensure that any value applied to that field conforms to the ISO standard.

DC types refine the definition of the core element itself. The basic DC element **date**, defined as "a date associated with an event in the life cycle of the resource" is too generic to be useful. By applying a type, the basic date element can be transformed into **date created, issued, accepted, available,** or **acquired,** among other possibilities. This ability to refine and enhance the schema without corrupting its fundamental nature and structure is the key to metadata extensibility. Without it, any metadata system will quickly become obsolete regardless of how well conceived and executed initially.

## *Where Do I Put It?*

Metadata can live in several different places. Traditionally, as with the card catalog, it has been recorded and stored separately from the object it describes with a pointer of some sort to the location of the information resource itself. This is often the case in content management and data warehouse systems. Information resources will be given a unique identifier and stored in whatever form and on whatever system is most appropriate. The metadata describing that resource may be hosted in a separate database dedicated to that purpose. The metadata and the object it describes remain linked by means of the resource's identifier.

This approach has the advantage of making it simple to update the metadata of any given information resource. If a new manager takes over responsibility for a large number of documents, you can simply update the database with the new information rather than tracking down and retagging the documents themselves. The disadvantage of this approach is that the metadata doesn't travel with the document if it is shared. If a file with externally managed metadata is emailed to a colleague at another organization, they will receive the content but not the descriptive information. This can become a problem if that additional information is critical to making the document usable.

An alternative to external management is to make the metadata a part of the information resource itself. Most applications supporting this approach store metadata as properties of the file they describe. Microsoft Windows, for example, allows an author to add summary metadata to any file, which may then be used to organize, locate, and retrieve the information resource. In addition to traveling with the file, internal metadata has the advantage of being somewhat self-maintaining. In the case of Windows metadata, some information is extracted directly and automatically from the document itself. The organization of the file is automatically extracted from heading styles in a Word document, Excel worksheet titles, or slide titles in a PowerPoint presentation. If the file changes, the new structure is automatically reflected in the metadata. Usage statistics are also automatically updated throughout the life of the document. At first blush, semi-automatic maintenance and close coupling with the information it describes makes internal metadata a very attractive option, but it does come at a cost.

First, while some of the descriptive metadata (*title, author, company*) can be automatically generated, the fields that are most useful to retrieval (*subject, category, keywords*) must be manually selected, keyed, and maintained. If the owner of the document changes, as mentioned earlier, not only does that field need to be updated in each impacted document, there will be no history of ownership. Once an internal field is updated, all previous values are lost. This can become critical if an explanation of something in the document is needed and no one remembers who originally wrote it.

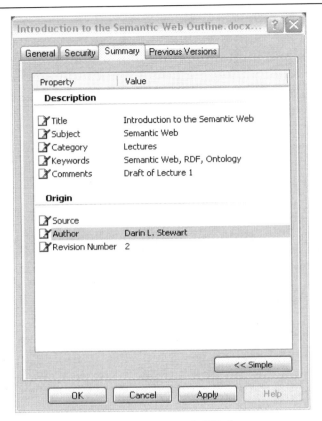

**Figure 5. Metadata in Microsoft Windows.**

Another hazard is shifting terminology. The vocabulary of any organization or community inevitably changes over time. Keywords, subject headings, and even category labels need to be updated to reflect these changes. Otherwise a search engine will not be able to match a relevant document tagged with obsolete terms with a query from a user searching with the latest buzzwords. Additionally, while deliberate keywords are essential to effective retrieval, as discussed in the prior chapter, the burden of selecting, assigning and maintaining them falls primarily on the author (who is invariably overworked already). This often leads to sporadic metadata and often idiosyncratic tags and terms. This becomes an even greater problem in the context of authority control, which we will discuss shortly.

# *Where Does It Come From?*

The potential sources of metadata and the means of creating it are as varied as the information resources they describe. Systems for automatic generation exist but rarely reach an acceptable level of quality without human assistance. Conversely, a broad application of metadata across an enterprise of any size is generally too tedious for human beings working without the help of scripts, term extractors and tagging tools. As a result, most successful metadata endeavors draw on a range of sources, tools and techniques depending on the nature of the information under consideration and the purposes for which it is intended.

The same principle is just as applicable to creating the metadata for a single information resource as it is to an entire collection. In most cases, the descriptive metadata will be assigned by the creator or author of the information. This has the advantage of terms coming from the person most familiar with the content and its original intent. It has the disadvantage of the metadata reflecting the biases and idiosyncrasies of the author, whose vocabulary may not necessarily reflect that of her audience.

The readers may also place the information in a different context from that originally conceived by the author. As a result, it is often advantageous to leave the creation of descriptive metadata to the professionals. The **National Information Standards Organization** (NISO) has noted that it is often more efficient to have indexers or other information professionals create this metadata, because the authors rarely have the time or necessary skills.[8] This is, of course, an additional line item cost, but when lifetime cost of ownership (especially in terms of findability) is taken into account, leaving it to the professionals is often cheaper in the long run.

Administrative and structural metadata will often be generated by the technical staff that prepares an information resource to be published and distributed. The individual scanning an image or creating a digital recording is in the best position to supply details about resolution, bit rates and encoding schemes. The individual adding the resource to the content management system will know when it is to be posted to the website, for how long, and where it is to be archived at the end of its run.

As with any budding field, there are an abundance of tools available to assist in the creation of metadata. The most common (and cheapest) is the application of templates such as those available in most word processing applications. In addition to providing standardized formatting of common document types, templates can also guide the author in providing basic descriptive metadata. Even if professional indexers are utilized to create the final metadata, it is often effective for the author to create a "first draft" of the metadata to serve as a guide. A well conceived document template can simplify this task and improve the quality of the metadata.

One of the challenges of high quality metadata is ensuring that it conforms to the appropriate schema. Mark-up and tagging tools can prompt the user for the appropriate fields, requiring those that are mandatory for compliance to the designated schema. Once the metadata is complete, the tool can either embed the metadata in the information resource itself or export it to an external metadata repository or database.

Extraction tools will analyze the content of an information resource and attempt to extract appropriate terms and values for certain metadata fields. For structural metadata, this is often straightforward and quite effective. For more conceptual elements such as subject, category or keyword, it gets a bit trickier. Most tools rely on a mixture of statistical and computational techniques to make a best guess at appropriate descriptive metadata. In most cases these tools require a great deal of training in terms of sample documents and target vocabularies, and still depend on human intervention and revision. However, much like having authors take a first pass at assigning metadata, automated extraction tools can dramatically reduce the full metadata burden to a more manageable one of cleanup and refinement.

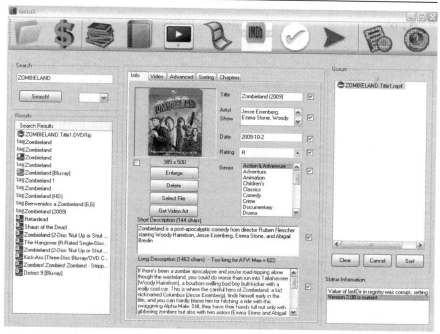

**Figure 6. A metadata creation aid: Meta-X.**

# *Metadata and Authority Control*

Metadata is a hard sell. It is expensive to create and difficult to maintain. Executives have a tough time understanding how the problem of having too much information to manage can be solved by adding on yet more information. Metadata is a bit of a "hair of the dog" solution. We add a little extra information to make a lot of information more usable. As to the expense the answer is, of course, pay now or pay more later; sometimes a lot more. As discussed in the prior chapter, a few moments tagging a document can save hours hunting for it later. When done properly, metadata initiatives nearly always generate a positive return on investment. Unfortunately, few are done properly and most fail. A prime reason for this is a lack of **authority control**.

The notion of authority control boils down to making sure everyone involved in the creation and management of an information resource is speaking the same language. It is the mechanism by which consistency in online systems is created and maintained. When applied to search and even navigation, it promotes greater precision by providing official or "authorized" forms of names, labels and values. As part of this system, references to equivalent terms and synonyms and variants are created which dramatically improve recall.[9] recall.[9] For example, if the authorized term for a "non-rigid, buoyant airship" is **blimp** there will be cross references to **zeppelin** and **dirigible**. An information seeker searching on any of these equivalent terms would receive information for all of them.

The value of authority control to metadata should be obvious. While schemas provide structure, syntax and semantics to our metadata, *they do nothing to ensure consistency in the values assigned to the elements of the schema.* The Dublin Core may specify an element called *language* and define it as, "the language of the intellectual content of the resource," but it does nothing to limit the potential values that can be assigned to that field. If DC metadata is being created for an international news story, its language could be tagged as **English, Eng., En, American English, British English,** or any number of variants. Each is potentially valid, but the lack of consistency turns retrieval into a crap shoot. If an information seeker searches on **English** they will receive only those information resources labeled with that exact term. Anything tagged with another term for English will be ignored.

The solution is to restrict potential metadata values to an agreed upon list of terms, so that both information creators and seekers are speaking the same language. In many cases, an authoritative vocabulary already exists and can be adopted wholesale. In the case of the DC language element, the International Organization for Standardization (ISO) Language Codes standard (ISO 639-2) provides authoritative names and codes for languages. English would then be consistently represented as **eng,** Italian as **ita,** Japanese as **jpn** and Esperanto as **epo.**

If the desired granularity does not exist in the standard, it can be expanded. DCMI actually recommends this as a best practice in the case of languages.[10] The ISO standard can be used in conjunction with the Internet Societies' proposal for language codes (RFC 3066), which includes the more specific labels of **en-US** for American English, **en-AU** for English as used in Australia, **en-GB** for English in the United Kingdom, or even **en-GB-oed** for British English using spelling from the Oxford English Dictionary. The additional advantage of adopting authoritative terms is the possibility of structuring the labels to reflect relationships.

    Eng(UseFor English, en,)
       En-AU (UseFor Australian English)
       En-GB (UseFor British English)
       En-GB-oed(UseFor British English OED spelling)

Despite the advantages it offers, authority control is a difficult pill to swallow for most organizations. The prospect of giving up ownership of terms and labels is often enough to incite turf battles in even the most collegial of environments. Authors feel that it is unnecessary and even inadvisable to constrain their vocabulary in any way (though they invariably recognize the need for such constraints among their colleagues). Deciding who and what is the "authority" and who and what is governed by its dictates are among the most contentious issues in information management. If metadata is a hard sell, authority control can turn into a shotgun wedding.

Fortunately, it needn't be so. A balance can be struck between the expressive needs of content authors and the findability needs of information seekers. Doing so depends on the proper definition, creation and management of the information resources provided to both groups. Taxonomies are the lynch pin of this process.

# 3

# Taxonomy

Everyone's a superhero.
Everyone's a Captain Kirk.
With orders to identify.
To clarify and classify...

Nena, "99 Red Balloons"

Human beings like things to be organized. We want to find carrots in the produce aisle, cornflakes in the cereal aisle and muffins in the bakery department. A gallon of milk on the magazine rack would strike us as somewhat amiss. As part of this preference for orderliness, we have a natural inclination to organize things ourselves. A quick glance at your desk may seem to dispute this assertion, but from the moment we wake up each morning, we begin breaking down the day into manageable chunks and sorting them into categories. Is it a weekend or a workday? If it is a workday, is it a productive day or a meeting day? If it's a meeting day, do you need to actively participate or just look attentive? How the pieces of the day get sorted into these categories will govern how you proceed. Do you roll over and go back to sleep, or do you get up and put on a tie?

This process is so basic and automatic that we are rarely aware that it is happening. We don't consciously classify music as "too loud." We just turn down the radio. Rather than compare the current room temperature against well defined criteria for "hot," "cold," and "comfortable," we simply adjust the thermostat. We are rarely aware that we are classifying, and yet we could not function without doing so. As George Lakoff puts it in his book *Women, Fire and Dangerous Things*, "There is nothing more basic than categorization to our thought, perception, action and speech."[1]

We each have in our head a system for sorting and labeling our world. Only very small portions of that system exist at a conscious level. For the most part, our categories have developed over the course of a lifetime with us blissfully unaware of how our experiences shape the way we organize our world. In general, our internal organizational schemes serve us well. Our desks may look cluttered, but we usually know what is in each pile and how to find what we need when we need it within our own domain.

Unfortunately, these personalized categories begin to break down as soon as other people become involved. "A pile for everything and everything in its pile" may work for me, but heaven help the person who needs to locate an invoice in my file cabinet or a memo on my hard drive. Every individual will have their own take on how a group of items should be sorted. Dump a silverware drawer on the table and ask three people to group the contents according to similarity and you are likely to get three different results. One individual may group them by material: wood, metal, plastic. A second may sort them into long utensils and short utensils. A third may classify them as formal versus casual. There is no reason to expect the contents of the drawer to be sorted neatly into separate piles of forks, knives and spoons, unless specific instructions are given to do so.

Even if categories are provided and the criteria for membership are defined, difficulties will often arise. Consider the "spork," a favorite utensil of fast food restaurants and convenience stores. Where does it belong in our silverware scheme? Spoon? Fork? How do you classify something that equally exhibits characteristics from two or more different categories? Such things are said to be **intertwingled**.

This odd word simply means that they are connected together in a complex way. Specifically, that they are composed of one another's components[2]. The term was coined by Ted Nelson in his book *Computer Lib*, where he wrote, "Intertwingularity is not generally acknowledged; people keep pretending they can make things deeply hierarchical, categorizable and sequential when they can't. Everything is deeply intertwingled."[3]

It is simple to sort clearly distinct items, such as black buttons from white buttons, but what do you do with the grey buttons? Usually, objects like this end up in an ungainly pile labeled

**The intertwingled spork.**

"other." This may seem like a sensible solution, until you realize that the contents of the "other" bucket outnumbers the contents of all other categories combined. The natural response to this conundrum is to create more and more specific categories. The danger here is in ending up with as many categories as items to classify. There is always a trade-off between precision of description and the number of groups one must keep straight. This is a difficult balance to find.

Clearly, classification is a messy business. As the amount of information to be managed grows, so does the complexity of the system needed to organize it. As the number of people who must access and interpret that information increases and becomes more diversified, the number of potential interpretations (and misinterpretations) grows exponentially. There comes a point when informal, ad hoc approaches to organization are no longer sustainable. To manage information in a sustainable manner that doesn't hamper information producers while still assisting information consumers, a more formal approach to organizing information is needed. Providing this formalization is the role of **enterprise taxonomy**.

# *Linnaean Taxonomy*

A **taxonomy** is simply a hierarchical collection of categories used to organize information. While it has roots dating back to Aristotle,[4] its modern usage began with **Carolus Linnaeus** (1707–1778), the "Father of Taxonomy." In 1735, Linnaeus published a thin pamphlet entitled *Systema Naturae* that described a system for grouping plants and animals according to shared physical characteristics. This pamphlet evolved into the **Linnaean Taxonomy** system of classification still in use today in the life sciences, albeit in greatly modified form.

## LINNAEAN TAXONOMY

|            | Human      | Dog         | Wolf        |
|------------|------------|-------------|-------------|
| **Kingdom** | Animalia   | Animalia    | Animalia    |
| **Phylum**  | Chordata   | Chordata    | Chordata    |
| **Class**   | Mammalia   | Mammalia    | Mammalia    |
| **Order**   | Primates   | Ungulculata | Ungulculata |
| **Family**  | Hominoidea | Carnivora   | Carnivora   |
| **Genus**   | Homo       | Canis       | Canis       |
| **Species** | Sapiens    | Familiari   | Lupus       |

**Figure 2.  Taxonomy according to Linnaeus.**

Linnaean taxonomy classifies nature into a seven level hierarchy: Kingdom, Phylum, Class, Order, Family, Genus, Species (see figure 2). Kingdoms are divided into Phylum, Phylum are divided into Classes, Classes into Orders and so on down through the final grouping of Species, creating a unique and singular designation. At higher levels of the taxonomy, things as seemingly different as a human being and a dog may be lumped together. At the Kingdom, Phylum and Class levels there is no difference between how a person and a pooch are classified. As you move down the hierarchy, the criteria for membership in a category becomes more precise and categories more discriminating. For example, a human and a dog diverge at the Order level, but a wolf and a domesticated dog do not split off until the Species level is reached. This hierarchical arrangement is very powerful as it lets you determine the level of discrimination between groups according to what best serves your own purposes.

The fundamental operating principle of traditional Linnean Taxonomy is "a place for everything and everything in its place." For the purposes of scientific classification, this is very useful. It would be problematic to have two bacteria, one beneficial, one lethal, with the same designation. When applied to the broader world of use, however, this rigid, singular classification breaks down.

---

### The Celestial Emporium of Benevolent Knowledge

Jorge Luis Borges often noted the difficulties of developing an objective classification scheme. He wrote, "It is clear that there is no classification of the Universe that is not arbitrary and full of conjectures." As an example he cited, "a certain Chinese encyclopedia entitled *Celestial Emporium of Benevolent Knowledge*. On those remote pages it is written that animals are divided into (a) those that belong to the Emperor, (b) embalmed ones, (c) those that are trained, (d) suckling pigs, (e) mermaids, (f) fabulous ones, (g) stray dogs, (h) those that are included in this classification, (i) those that tremble as if they were mad, (j) innumerable ones, (k) those drawn with a very fine camel's hair brush, (l) others, (m) those that have just broken a flower vase, (n) those that resemble flies from a distance."

—*"The Analytical Language of John Wilkins*

Depending on your perspective or current purpose, any given item could easily fit into multiple categories. While a German Shepherd can rightly be designated as **canis familiari**, a nine year old is more likely to think of it as a family pet. A cattle rancher would lump it in with his other work animals and a blind person may classify it as a service animal. Each classification is valid from the perspective of the person utilizing the resource, in this case a dog, for their own purpose. Consider also the differing sensibilities among various audiences and communities. A German Shepherd could be classified as either a work animal or a food animal with equal validity. In Western cultures, this is distasteful at best. In Eastern cultures, it is self-evident.

Modern taxonomy has expanded beyond the Linnaean model to accommodate these complexities. It is no longer intended as a means to restrict terms and labels, but rather as a mechanism to manage their use and to ensure the availability of information. There are several approaches to achieving this goal, ranging in levels of complexity and amount of control. All of these strategies, including taxonomy, may be thought of as some flavor of **controlled vocabulary**.

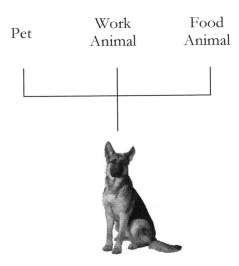

Pet        Work          Food
           Animal        Animal

**Figure 3. Views and sensibilities may vary
by region and culture.**

# *Controlled Vocabularies*

In the most basic sense, a **controlled vocabulary** is nothing more than a **nomenclature**, a standardized set of terms and phrases used to describe a subject area or information domain. Most often, these preferred terms form an **indexing language** that is used to assist in more precise retrieval of content. Such a language enables an item or concept to be labeled in a way that a group of individuals can be assured that they are all talking about the same thing when using a particular word or phrase. However, restricting people to communicating with only an authorized vocabulary has certain Orwellian overtones that may be at best unpalatable and at worst unacceptable. To overcome this, a variety of controlled vocabulary types exist each with its own level of complexity and degree of control.

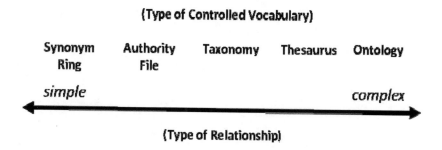

The first step toward enhancing the flexibility of a restricted vocabulary is the addition of **equivalence relationships**. Term equivalencies are usually first encountered by high school essayists attempting to embellish their vocabularies by consulting Dr. Peter M. Roget's catalog of synonymy (also known as Roget's Thesaurus). In the context of information retrieval, the purpose of equivalence lists, more properly called **synonym rings**, is to associate all known variations of a given term so that regardless of which term is used in a query, any document containing an equivalent term will also be retrieved.

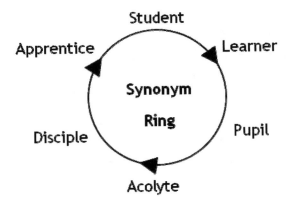

It is important to note that in this context, equivalency relationships are defined for "purposes of retrieval" and so may not represent true equivalencies in a natural language sense. Synonyms, near-synonyms, acronyms, abbreviations, and lexical variants are all valid candidates for inclusion in a synonym ring. Common misspellings may also be included in synonym rings, allowing spelling-challenged searchers to find "chedder" as well as "cheddar" cheese.

While synonym rings make life much simpler for the end user, they tend to complicate things for the information manager and system developer by complicating queries and lookup tables. To simplify

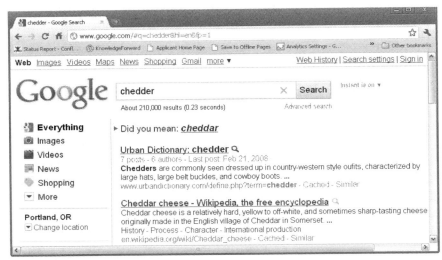

**Figure 4. Synonyms in Google.**

things and promote consistent labeling of information, a synonym ring should usually be enhanced to become an authority file.

An **authority file** is simply a synonym ring with a single term identified as the **preferred term** or the acceptable value. In the example shown in the figure below, "student" may be identified in the authority file as the preferred term. As such, it should always be used by system developers, product managers and marketing staff to represent the concept "a person formally engaged in learning." While this usage may be enforced among employees, customers are unlikely to feel so constrained. They will still use whatever term they prefer when searching for information. These other terms should still be available as **entry terms** into the vocabulary that lead users to the preferred term. An authority file will work behind the scenes, by means of operators such as USE, USE FOR, or simply UF, to translate these non-standard search terms into the official term employed by the system.

```
Student USE FOR Pupil, Learner, Acolyte,
    Disciple, Apprentice

Apprentice USE Student

Learner USE Student

Student UF Disciple
```

**Figure 5. Preferred term relationships.**

Determination of a preferred term cannot be done arbitrarily. It must be done with significant consideration and should be supported with evidence of how the term is currently used. A justification of this sort constitutes a **user warrant** and determines how a term should be handled based on how users are accustomed to applying it. If one of the terms used to represent a concept stands out from the others because of its frequent use in searches or information requests, it is a prime candidate for preferred term.

While synonym rings and authority files can greatly enhance the performance of search engines, they do little to guide and inform the information seeker. As discussed in Chapter One, users often do not have a clear picture of the question they are trying to answer or the nature of the answer they are seeking when they set out on a search for information. Put simply, they don't know what they don't know. This highlights a shortcoming of synonym rings and authority files. These rings and files have no structure beyond that of a simple list. Consequently, they cannot provide any context to the user or help them articulate their information need. To provide this extra guidance, the hierarchical structure of a taxonomy is needed.

A taxonomy encapsulates three basic types of hierarchical relationships: *is a type of,* e.g. a German Shepherd *is a type of* dog; *is a part of,* a toe *is a part of* a foot; and *is an instance of,* e.g. Portland *is an instance of* a city. Theses parent/child relationships expressed in the hierarchical organization of a traditional Linnean taxonomy are a powerful tool for helping an information seeker refine their information need. If they are not finding enough information with a particular term, they can move one step up the hierarchy, say from "dog" to "pet," and receive much broader results. Conversely, if they receive too many matching results, they can move down the hierarchy to a narrower category, moving from "dog" to "cocker spaniel," zeroing in on the precise information they need. While this strict progression of broadening and narrowing categories is a great strength of traditional taxonomy, it is also an Achilles' heel when intertwingledness rears its ugly head. Information does not always neatly fit into a single category. Certain items will often find an equally appropriate home in several categories. Take for example the book, *The Mormon Graphic Image, 1834 –1914: Cartoons, Caricatures, and Illustrations.*[5] Does this belong under "Americana," "Religion," "History of the Press," "Religious History," or "Humor"? If the book is to be placed in a single slot and the person doing the categorization has a different mindset or bias than the user of the taxonomy, it is likely that this book will never be found again.

To avoid these pitfalls, enterprise taxonomies are often **poly-hierarchical**; that is, a given item of interest may be represented by multiple nodes of the taxonomy. Put another way, any term in the hierarchy may have more than one parent term. What this translates to in practical application is multiple paths to any piece of information. This may seem to violate the taxonomic principle of "a place for everything and everything in its place," but it may be necessary to meet the demands of information seekers.

**Figure 6. Where does this book belong?**

For example, one of the most common applications of enterprise taxonomies currently is support of website navigation. When one considers the various and complex ways in which the pages making up a corporate website interact, it should become obvious that the traditional Linnaean taxonomy, with its single location for any item, is not up to the task. Few users will tolerate being forced to follow a rigid, predetermined path to the information they are after. If the user wants to find their way to a book on mushrooms by drilling down under "vegetarian meals", let her. If she is more likely to find the topic by navigating a branch on the "psychedelic movement of the 1960s", provide that avenue as well. A poly-hierarchical approach to taxonomy can accommodate both.

To illustrate, consider the tomato. In a traditional taxonomy a tomato is a fruit; end of story. This classification may not sit well with certain third graders who know beyond any doubt that a tomato is a vegetable. To reconcile these two factions, the tomato is placed in

# TRADITIONAL TAXONOMY

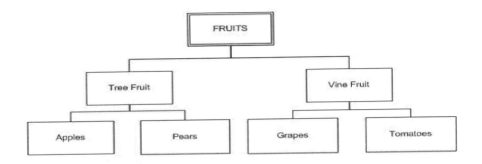

# POLY-HIERARCHICAL TAXONOMY

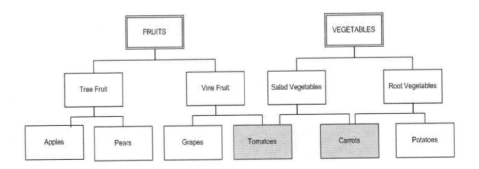

both the Fruit branch and the Vegetable branch of the taxonomy as depicted in Figure 9.[7] Once the step into poly-hierarchy is taken, the hierarchical structure of the taxonomy begins to transform into more of a lattice-like structure. This lattice is the beginning of the next step up the controlled vocabulary food chain: **thesauri**.

While the core structure of a thesaurus is still hierarchical, the tree structure expands to include the notion of **related terms**. Concepts may be related in many ways beyond the parent/child relationship of broader and narrower terms and basic synonymy. While a "corkscrew" is not a more general or specific version of a "table wine" the two are definitely related. A thesaurus allows these two concepts to be explicitly associated with one another without losing the benefits of hierarchical organization.

The three most common relationships, hierarchical, equivalence and associative comprise the **standard thesaural relationships.**[8] In addition to these three foundational relationships, several structural relationships are available to increase the flexibility and functionality of a thesaurus.

> **Scope Note**: A note attached to a term to indicate its meaning within an indexing language.
>
> **Use**: The term that follows the symbol is the preferred term when a choice between synonyms or quasi-synonyms exists.
>
> **Use For**: The term that follows the symbol is a non-preferred synonym or quasi-synonym.
>
> **Top Term**: The term that follows the symbol is the name of the broadest class to which the specific concept belongs; sometimes used in the alphabetical section of a thesaurus.
>
> **Broader Term**: The term that follows the symbol represents a concept having a wider meaning.

**Narrower Term**: The term that follows the symbol refers to a concept with a more specific meaning.

**Related Term**: The term that follows the symbol is associated, but is not a synonym, a quasi-synonym, a broader term or a narrower term.

The main use of thesauri is to move the facility of a controlled vocabulary beyond simple content navigation and term standardization into expanded search and retrieval enhancement. As the Ark Group puts it, thesauri are for improving the performance of the index at the back of the book using synonyms and standardized hierarchies of preferred, broader and narrower terms, while taxonomies are about organizing the content of the book in the first place.[9]

A thesaurus can be presented in several ways. The traditional flat view shown in figure 10 is the simplest and most common. This view can present difficulties, however, as in the example above where only the heading terms, "geologic contacts" and "geologic history" are available as entry points into the vocabulary. This demonstrates the necessity for mapping synonyms, turning the flat view into a **rotated** or **permuted list** displaying all words used in the thesaurus. This allows a searcher to enter the thesaurus using any word from either a formal thesaurus entry term or a synonym. Without additional entry terms, the additional information available from the thesaurus is invisible to anyone using a variant term.

Going one step further, a **multilevel thesaurus** adopts the tree structure familiar from taxonomies and displays all levels its hierarchical relationships. Finally, term relationships can also be shown graphically as a network of nodes. The difficulty with graphical representations of this sort is that the intersecting lines of the map are often so dense that individual relationships cannot be visually teased out by the user without great effort. Most thesauri currently in use today stick to the more traditional, paper-like representations with the possible exception of including hyperlinks between heading and entry terms.

```
geologic contacts
SN: Plane or irregular surface between two types
or ages of rock; examples are faults, intrusive
borders, bedding planes separating distinct
strata, and unconformities.
        [Glossary of Geology, 4th ed.]
BT: stratigraphic sections
NT: unconformities
RT: stratigraphy
UF: contacts (geologic)

geologic history
SN: Record (and inferred reconstruction) of the
origin and development of the Earth since its
formation.
BT: Earth characteristics
NT: biostratigraphy
Earth history
l ithostratigraphy
RT: geologic time scales
geology
paleontology
paleoseismology
stratigraphy
UF: chronostratigraphy
geohistory
```

**Figure 7. Example thesaurus entries.**

# *Faceted Classification*

Each type of the controlled vocabulary we have discussed so far is an **enumerative classification scheme**. That is, they attempt to list all possible subjects present in the area they are intended to organize and represent. Traditionally, they are created in a more or less top-down manner, defining categories and then assigning items where they best fit. A wine merchant would divide his potential wares into Red, White, Pink and Bubbly. Each type would then be further divided: Red into Cabernet Sauvignon, Merlot, Pinot Noir and Zinfandel; White into Chardonnay, Semillon and Riesling; Bubbly into Champagne and Sparkling. When a new bottle is added to the inventory, it is compared to this list of available categories and shelved according to the best fit.

This approach works well for the warehouse manager, interested primarily in keeping his shelves orderly, but what about the customer looking for a Riesling from the Sonoma Valley or an Australian Grenache for under $20? The information available in the simple wine-types hierarchy above is of little help in zeroing in on the specific bottle we are seeking. These other dimensions (region, price and the like) are essential to finding the right product unless the customer is willing to examine every label on every bottle of wine.

Just as a map that shows only longitude would be of little use to a navigator, a taxonomy that only accounts for one aspect of a subject is of little use to an information seeker. As W.B. Sayer notes:

> A classification's task is to provide for the field of knowledge or part of it, as comprehensive and clear a statement as the cartographer is able to make of a territory of the earth, for just as a map makes clear the relationship between place and place, so a classification strives to show the relationship of each branch of knowledge to the other branches.[10]

This is a tall order for a single hierarchy of categories and is a major weakness of traditional taxonomy and even a poly-hierarchical taxonomy. How do you accommodate all the different aspects of a topic that may be of interest? What if the scope of a subject grows or even shrinks once the hierarchy is developed? Can you add in new branches without disrupting the entire tree?

S.R. Ranganathan, generally considered the greatest librarian of the twentieth century, commented on the strengths and limitations of enumerative approaches to classification in his book, *Philosophy of Library Classification.*

An enumerative scheme ... can be suitable and even economical for a closed system of knowledge. ... What distinguishes the universe of current knowledge is that it is a dynamical continuum. It is ever growing; new branches may stem from any of its infinity of points at any time; they are unknowable at present. They cannot therefore be enumerated here and now; nor can they be anticipated. Their filiations can be determined only after they appear.[11]

To accommodate the ever expanding "universe of current knowledge," Ranganathan developed an alternative system based on **facets**. Linguistically, the word facet derives from the French *facette* meaning "little face," as in one of the polished surfaces of a cut gem. Just as a diamond has many facets so does any given subject, each representing a different view, aspect, or dimension. Ranganathan devised a scheme, **colon classification**, that allowed all pertinent facets of an item to be represented in its classification.

Rather than defining a single hierarchy that represents one view of a subject, faceted classification identifies several mutually exclusive categories and provides a hierarchy for each. The online wine and spirits store wine.com is an excellent example of faceted classification. As shown on the next page, facets are provided for Wine Type, Region and Price. Each of these dimensions may be used to identify and purchase a particular wine, meeting the customer's specific requirements. Suppose I am looking for a red wine from an Oregon vineyard costing between $20 and $40. The faceted classification system employed by wine.com can translate this request into the exact coordinates for a 2004 Pinot Noir from Ponzi Vineyards in the Willamette Valley.

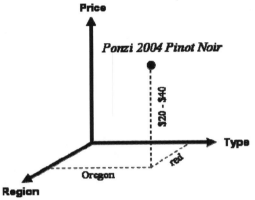

Ranganathan identified five basic facets he believed could adequately represent any subject or object.

| | |
|---|---|
| **Personality** | What the object is about, the main subject or topic. |
| **Material** | What the object is made of. |
| **Energy** | What happens to the object, the activity or process. |
| **Space** | Where that action takes place or where the object exists. |
| **Time** | When the action takes place or where the object occurs. |

Referred to in library circles by the acronym **PMEST,** these facets fit together like puzzle pieces to describe any given subject. For example, a book on "the design of wooden furniture in eighteenth-century America" would utilize all five of the PMEST facets in its description. Furniture is the central topic or Personality; the Material used is wood, the process (Energy facet) is design, the design occurs in America and so fills the Space facet, leaving Time as the eighteenth century.[12]

While Ranganathan's PMEST facets have proven extremely robust since their first application in the 1930s, they are by no means required. Appropriate facets will be derived directly from the information you are attempting to organize. Faceted classification turns the traditional process of creating a controlled vocabulary on its head. Rather than starting at the top and creating a priori categories and then slotting items into them, facet analysis begins bottom-up with the items to be classified themselves, pulling out their most essential and persistent characteristics. These are then marshaled into hierarchies for each facet. To a certain extent, this eliminates the need for poly-hierarchies, as these facets tend to be orthogonal and mutually exclusive to each other.

Rather than creating multiple paths through a single hierarchy, an object can be associated with elements from multiple hierarchies. This allows a user to both jump to the desired item by providing coordinates (Red Wine, Oregon, $20–$40) or to navigate through any of the facets of interest. This is a powerful combination. Individuals can develop a detailed shared understanding of a subject or a particular item within a subject in terms of its features as represented by these mutually exclusive facets.

Facets need not be restricted to the information being managed. They may also be used to represent the users of that information. For example, a corporate Intranet may use a Personality facet such as "Subject Matter" to represent the main topic of a document and also present a "Role" facet to indicate the primary audience for that document. This provides an additional level of discrimination for the information seeker. The range of facets that can be applied are limited only to their usefulness to the particular audience they are intended to serve.

This has implications beyond the organizational structure. As Barbara Kwasnick points out:

> Faceted classifications are not really a different representational structure but rather a different approach to the classification process. The notion of facets rests on the belief that there is more than one way to view the world, and that even those classifications that are viewed as stable are in fact provisional and dynamic. The challenge is to build classifications that are flexible and can accommodate new phenomena.[13]

In addition to its considerable descriptive power, faceted classification has the advantage of readily accommodating new additions to its structure as the scope of a subject expands. This eliminates the need to imagine all possible and potential categories in advance and the difficulties of shoe-horning new categories in after the fact.

This power comes at a price. The ease with which new facets can be added to a classification scheme and existing facets can be expanded makes it easy for things to get out of control. In some cases a user may prefer to add an ad hoc facet rather than buy into the agreed upon vocabulary. As the facet structure grows more and more free-form, it becomes less and less useful. Even if the faceted vocabulary is well managed, deciding what constitutes a good facet can be tricky. If you classify according to trivial characteristics, you will find only trivial information. What happens when terminology changes and an existing facet no longer makes sense?

These questions are at the core of taxonomy development and need to be answered before the first category is defined. Without a clear roadmap of how a taxonomy will be developed and maintained, you will not make it beyond the sticky-notes-on-the-white-board phase.

# 4

# Preparations

...there is nothing more difficult to plan, more doubtful of success, nor more dangerous to manage than the creation of a new system. For the initiator has the enmity of all who profit by the preservation of the old institution and merely lukewarm defenders in those who would gain by the new one.

Machiavelli, The Prince, 1513

Creating a taxonomy, or a controlled vocabulary of any sort, is a very situation-specific endeavor. Audience, content, sponsorship, technology, compliance requirements, budget, and schedule are all factors that will influence not only the end product, but the development process itself. As a result, there is no single correct and proper way to create a taxonomy. Despite this, there are general principles and basic phases that are common to nearly all taxonomy projects. These may be grouped as the "Three Cs" and the "Five Phases."

Every controlled vocabulary must reconcile three often opposing forces: Content, Community and Context. These are the "Three Cs." First and foremost is the **content** that the taxonomy is meant to organize and support. The source material with which you will be working will provide the raw materials for creating your new vocabulary. These documents can be your most valuable asset but can also pose some formidable challenges. In most situations, the content you must corral will be spread across multiple repositories ranging from file servers to filing cabinets to forgotten stacks of paper in a cubicle. Most of this content will be unstructured, likely redundant or out of date, and quite volatile. There is also likely to be a lot of it.

Depending on the scope of the project, the amount of content will likely range from a few file directories tied to a single website up to multiple offsite storage facilities packed with banker boxes of files. As you pick your way through the enterprise's content holdings, you will notice how many types of content, varying in form, substance and quality, for which you must account. All of this content does not necessarily need to be included in the development process. The decision of what is in or out of scope, however, must be an explicit and documented choice. To make these decisions valid, you must account for the **community**.

The community consists of those individuals for whom the taxonomy is being built. These stakeholders may not always be of the human variety. Software agents and engines may be the primary beneficiaries of your controlled vocabulary, and as such must have their needs taken into account. To ensure adequate representation of all interests, it is essential to determine who exactly your stakeholders are. These people may not be direct users of the final product, but may still have a stake in the project. Stakeholders of this sort may include executive sponsors, external content providers, IT support staff, and others.

As your list of community members lengthens, different **audiences**, or groupings of individuals with common interests, will become apparent. The characteristics that will define these audiences generally boil down to a single question: What do they *want* from this collection of content? Through your interactions with these audiences, you must take that question a step further to determine what it is they actually *need* from the collection. An understanding of this distinction may require a reallocation of stakeholders to audiences along with some sales work to convince them of what they actually need as opposed to what they perceive they need. Additional patterns will begin to emerge as you dig into their information-access behaviors. Commonalities in search, navigation, and retrieval habits will further refine your audience definitions.

Once your audience is defined, it is essential to prioritize them. Not all audiences will be equally important to the sponsor, and with limited resources, the taxonomy cannot be all things to all people. A variation on the Pareto principle is a good rule of thumb here: eighty percent of the users will have their needs met by twenty percent of the content in the collection. Similarly, eighty percent of your stakeholders will be contained in only twenty percent of your identified audiences. Meeting the needs of the eighty percent is a good rough cut at prioritization. Other factors that will refine your prioritization will be found by articulating the **context** of the taxonomy project.

Taxonomies do not exist in a vacuum. The environment in which they are created and maintained is a powerful factor in the success or failure of any such project. Contextual factors go beyond the obvious constraints of budget, technology, resources and schedule. Corporate culture and departmental dynamics must be considered along with business models and goals. Controlled vocabularies can be among the most politically charged endeavors any institution can undertake. Without accounting for corporate culture, history, and dynamics, the project will fail.

These three factors (content, community, and context) will not be fully understood at the outset of the project and will likely not be completely explored even by its end. Despite this, it is essential to keep them constantly in mind throughout the various phases of the project as they will influence the overall shape and progress of the taxonomy development cycle. At the highest level, this cycle can be divided into five phases: research, strategy, design, implementation, and administration.

# *The Taxonomy Development Cycle*

The foundational information for each of the Three Cs will be uncovered in the **research** phase of the project. During this period, you will start gathering information from every channel available to you. To begin to understand the information collection with which you will be working, you will need to conduct a **content audit**. The audit consists of a survey or sampling of the information materials from which the taxonomy will be built and which it will ultimately govern. It will provide a sense of what exactly you are dealing with in terms of the types of documents, their quality, format, volume, and volatility. It will also give you a baseline set of **terms** and **categories** from which to start the design of your controlled vocabulary.

During the research phase you must also get to know your stakeholders and audiences. This is usually accomplished through extensive interviews and group meetings. Out of these meetings and interviews, the taxonomist should start to get a sense for the context of the project as well. While critical contextual information must be fed into the documentation and planning of the project, it can be valuable to keep some of the more political information to oneself and let it guide and inform your actions as the project unfolds. This will avoid a great deal of unnecessary saber rattling and chest thumping while still accounting for these factors.

With research findings in hand, the project segues into the **strategy** phase. It is not necessary to have comprehensive and exhaustive research information prior to beginning formulation of a taxonomy strategy. In fact, it is unwise to wait for definitive conclusions, since the strategy will inform research efforts and vice versa. The two phases are complementary and should be approached in an iterative and cyclical manner. The goal of the strategy phase is to bridge the gap between research and development. It does so by making high-level decisions about the project. The organizational structure of the taxonomy should be determined as should the organizational scheme. The critical decision of buy or build must also be made at this point. If a build decision is made, or even a buy and modify approach, the decision must be made to take a top-down, bottom-up or hybrid approach to taxonomy creation. Recommendations pertaining to technologies, document identifiers, metadata scope and design, and many other aspects of the project are also made in this phase. Each of these choices is articulated and documented in a formal **governance document.**

The governance document will become the bible of the **design** and **implementation** phases of the taxonomy project. Most of the actual "work" of taxonomy development occurs in these two phases. The design phase transforms the lofty thinking and visionary goals of the strategy phase into an executable plan. This plan specifies what is to be delivered, what it will look like, how long it will take, who will do the work, who will use it when it's done, and a host of other details. The design phase will involve the application of any number of tools and techniques, including content mapping, blueprints and wire frames, content models, and eventually prototypes. Once the prototypes and design specifications have been approved by all relevant authorities, the project moves into the implementation phase, where the actual controlled vocabulary and its supporting system are built and integrated with the content it supports.

The final phase of taxonomy creation, **administration,** is perhaps the most difficult. It is at this point that you finally realize, or at least begin to appreciate, that a controlled vocabulary is never "done." Once deployed, a taxonomy must be continually monitored and updated. As new terms are discovered, they must be reconciled with the existing structure. As term meanings shift, new definitions will need to be reflected. Except in the rarest of circumstances, each of these changes will require the consensus of the primary taxonomy audiences.

## Stages of Taxonomy Development

**Figure 1. The Taxonomy Development Cycle**

In each iteration of the taxonomy development cycle, these phases will expand or contract due to the nature of the change. Following the overall pattern, however, will avoid missteps that could jeopardize the entire endeavor.

# *Research*

The primary goal of the research phase is to understand the environment the taxonomy must support. That environment is comprised of the three Cs mentioned earlier: Community, Content and Context. In practical terms, this means investigating and documenting the people, organizations, processes, content, and technologies that fall within the scope of the project. As a rule of thumb, always start with the people.

Structured interviews can inform the entire research phase by not only orienting the taxonomy designer to the organization, but by also establishing relationships that will be critical in the later phases of the project and can ultimately determine success or failure. The most important relationship to establish is with the project sponsor. This should always be your first meeting. In that meeting you must determine what precisely are the sponsor's goals for the project and how success will be determined and measured. You must also ensure that there is a common understanding of what a taxonomy or controlled vocabulary of any flavor actually is. This may involve some education work on the taxonomist's part. It is often useful to precede this critical meeting with some preparatory information including an executive summary of what a taxonomy is and has to offer. Do not expect this document actually to be read by the sponsor prior to your meeting, but it will provide points of reference and discussion during the ninety-second introduction to taxonomies you will provide at that first meeting.

You should also provide a brief list of questions that you want to cover with the sponsor. In addition to goals and success criteria, you should formulate questions around how this individual personally locates and accesses information, what that frequently accessed content is, and what are her biggest frustrations surrounding locating and retrieving documents. You should also ask how much of her budget is tied up in content support. The person likely will be unable to answer this question, but it will get her thinking in terms of the money you are going to save her. This is an important point when it comes time to discuss funding for the project.

A delicate question, but one the needs to be asked, is: "Has anything like this been attempted here before?" If so, you need to understand what worked, what didn't work, and why you are attempting it now. Often, efforts will have been attempted in the past and failed due to improper scoping, lack of understanding of what a controlled vocabulary can and can't do, and how to administer one. Most likely, the project imploded under the weight of corporate politics. Tread carefully through this area, but don't let the sponsor get off with easy and trivial answers. If there are known pitfalls, identify them upfront and circumvent them.

Finally, you need to determine who the sponsor thinks you should meet with next. This will help you reaffirm the scope of the project. If the original understanding was that the project is restricted to the human resources department and the sponsor sends you of to meet with the head of accounting and the director of marketing, you will need to clarify that this is to determine how those departments feed into human resources rather than how the taxonomy can accommodate their content as a separate domain. This is also a good opportunity to gauge the level of commitment the sponsor feels and the amount of support you can expect. It is important that the sponsor understand that creating a taxonomy is a time-intensive process that involves input from many people. She needs to be prepared to have people accept meeting invitations you send and free up resources as necessary. Without a clear commitment to this upfront, the project is in trouble before the kick-off meeting has even been scheduled. That kick-off meeting is the next step.

With the sponsor's initial list of stakeholders in hand, schedule a ninety-minute meeting with those individuals, including the sponsor, whose attendance is critical. In this kick-off meeting, repeat your ninety-second introduction to taxonomies, elaborating as necessary, to again make sure everyone understands what you are taking about. State the scope and goals of the project as articulated by the sponsor. It is important to state that this not as a fiat, but is more of a draft for which you would like their input and suggestions. This will promote a sense of ownership among the people whose calendars you are going to be dominating over the weeks to come. It is also important to establish a rough timeline for the project including milestones and deliverables. Milestones may include items such as "first round of interviews complete," "project scope document complete," "taxonomy framework draft ready for review," "initial categories defined" and so forth. In a project with often intangible benefits, it is essential to show concrete progress throughout. Milestones, if met, will demonstrate this progress.

The kick-off meeting should be followed by a series of individual and group meetings. In addition to those stakeholders identified by the sponsor, any others recommended in the kick-off meeting should also be scheduled. These interviews should be conducted as soon after the kick-off as possible while still providing the interviewee with sufficient time to prepare. Prior to the interviews you should provide them with the list of questions you covered with the sponsor, but refined and expanded to reflect the interests of the interview at hand. You should catalog what content dependencies exist for the stakeholder and his department. This includes who they receive content and documents from and to whom they provide content. These dependencies will often cross not only departmental boundaries, but the boundaries of the institution itself. Content service subscriptions and inter-agency collaborations are becoming extremely common and must be taken into account. The nature of these dependencies will also have an influence on the nature of the content itself. From those dependencies, develop an exhaustive list of the types of content on which the stakeholder and his constituents depend. Identify what forms, memos, reports, websites and documents are essential to their business function and begin to sort them into rough categories. This list along with similar lists from other stakeholders will form the basis of the content audit you will perform later.

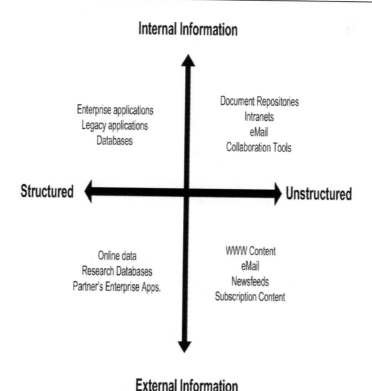

**Internal Information**

Enterprise applications
Legacy applications
Databases

Document Repositories
Intranets
eMail
Collaboration Tools

**Structured** ◄──────────────────────► **Unstructured**

Online data
Research Databases
Partner's Enterprise Apps.

WWW Content
eMail
Newsfeeds
Subscription Content

**External Information**

Often there will be a formal content management system in place, either for the department or the enterprise as a whole. If this is the case, determine who in the department is responsible for the system and how it is used. The same applies for any IT the department depends on for its content. Inventory the tools the individual or group use to prepare or utilize content. This ranges from Microsoft Office applications to content workflow suites. Find out who is the guru of those tools and systems or what team is responsible for them, and schedule a meeting to become familiar with their capabilities and quirks. It is often these tools that generate the metadata with which your taxonomy will be built and sustained. At the very least, you will discover any technical constraints within which you must work.

An invaluable and yet often overlooked source of information is Standard Operating Procedure documents (SOPs). If these policy manuals exist, they can give you tremendous insights into how an area is supposed to run, even if reality departs significantly from those policies. Often, attempts at term standardization have been made within these SOPs and can inform the structure of your taxonomy. They will also give you additional context and history for the project and environment.

At the conclusion of your interviews you should have a solid understanding of the community and who are the more prominent citizens. These core individuals should be recruited as a steering committee to serve not only as advisors to the project but as key communication channels back into the various constituencies. You should also have a good grasp on the general nature and extent of the content with which you will be dealing. Ideally, you will have an initial list of candidate terms for the first draft of your taxonomy. This is a significant milestone and prepares you to move on to the next step of the research phase: a **content audit**.

## *Performing a Content Audit*

Taxonomies are built *for* people, hence the importance of research interviews to understand the needs of those users. Taxonomies are built *from* content, so it naturally follows that the source content must be understood at least as well as user needs. You need to know what content the organization has, who is responsible for it, where it is and in what form, how it got there, and most importantly, who cares. This level of understanding is gained by performing a **content audit**.

It is important to make a clear distinction between a content audit and a **content inventory**. An audit is representative of the document and content collection as a whole and is based on directed sampling of sources identified in the stakeholder interviews. A content inventory is an exhaustive cataloging of every document and scrap of content within the scope of the taxonomy project. Even a small organization will usually have thousands, if not tens of thousands, of documents and a vast array of electronic and Web-based content. This amount of material is daunting even to the most intrepid taxonomist and has killed many projects before they are even fully launched. Fortunately, for the purposes of taxonomy design and creation, it is not necessary to account for every document or Web page ever created in the organization. Instead, it is essential to zero in on a new set of three Cs: **Critical Core Content**.

During the interview phase, the stakeholders should have identified what content they depend on to do their jobs and keep their organizations running. This group of documents and information sources will likely represent about twenty percent of the total content in that user's domain, again proving out the Pareto principal. For example, the stakeholders as a group may identify certain marketing, finance, and human resources documents as important to their business functions. If there are 20,000 total documents in these categories, as estimated from your interviews,[1] roughly 4,000 of these will actually be **core** content. Even 4,000 documents can still be overwhelming, so it is important to identify a manageable starting point. To do so, return to your stakeholders with the list of their core content and work with them to identify what content is **critical**. In other words, what content would cause work to halt if it were not available. This can most easily be accomplished by ranking documents in order of importance. With that ranked list, select the top twenty percent as the initial target for a content audit. You have reduced the scope of the audit from 20,000 documents you must review to a very manageable 800 (see table 1).

| Business Area | Total Documents | Core Content | Critical Content |
|---|---|---|---|
| Marketing | 5,000 | 1,000 | 200 |
| Finance | 10,000 | 2,000 | 400 |
| Human Resources | 5,000 | 1,000 | 200 |
| Total | 20,000 | 4,000 | 800 |

Table 1.  Reduce the scope of content that is to be audited.

Throughout this phase of the project, you should always be looking
for ROT: content that is Redundant, Obsolete or Trivial. Weeding
out this content will not only reduce the amount of material to be
reviewed and managed, it will keep the taxonomy streamlined and
focused on core functionality.

As you start pulling folders from filing cabinets and trolling the
company Intranet for content to assess, you must structure the
information you are hoping to extract. The nature and extent of this
metadata will depend largely on the goals and scope of the project.
There are, however, seven basic facets that are common to most
content audits. These are: Content, Category, Source, Location,
Stakeholder, Organization, and Term. These entities are interrelated,
and the associations among them must be identified and
documented. The simplest way to visualize this is as a simple data
model. This also lends itself to the creation of a trivial database
application to manage the information you glean from the collection.

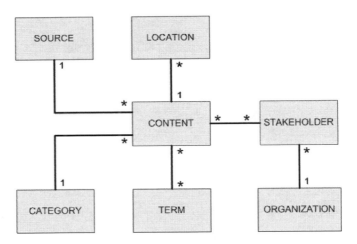

**Figure 2.  A simple content model.**

**Content**, of course, represents the material being examined itself.
This can be a hardcopy document, a dynamically generated report
from a data warehouse or operational database, a website, an alert
from a news feed—the list goes on and on. The point is, do not

exclude any source of content that a stakeholder deems critical just because it doesn't come packaged in a format you were expecting. The only exception to this rule is if that particular format *explicitly* falls outside the scope of the project. The information you need to collect about the content item at hand will populate most of the remaining entities in the content model as described below. In addition to this information, you must assign a unique identifier to the particular document instance you are currently examining. This identifier must be both accessible and comprehensible to a user—in this case you the taxonomist and your core team. It is also useful to provide a brief textual description of the item.

The identifiers, both machine generated and humanly readable, are useful in documenting dependencies among content. If a report references a key document necessary to its interpretation or distribution, you should note this dependency and create a new content entry for the referenced document. This is a perilous course, however, in that your 800 critical core documents could balloon into an unmanageable number. You may indicate in your entry that the document is referenced and leave it at that. In most cases, this placeholder is sufficient for the initial pass and can serve as a reminder in later phases. You also need an indication of the stability of the content—a measure of its volatility. Is this a report that is updated nightly, or is it a mission statement that hasn't been revised for decades? This information is critical to the maintenance of the deployed taxonomy.

The content should be assigned to a **category** that serves to group similar types of content into classes. An initial pool of categories will have presented itself from the stakeholder interviews, but you may find it necessary to add additional groups as you become more familiar with the content. Common categories include: Invoice, Purchase Order, Compliance Documentation, Personnel Action Form, Meeting Minutes, Procedural Documentation, and Correspondence. In this early stage of the project, it is important to resist the urge to break down or pool together categories more than is necessary. For example, Correspondence could easily be broken down into Internal and External. External could be split into

Supplier, Partner and Customer. Customer could be divided into Complaint, Compliment, Request and Inquiry. Similarly, Personnel Action Form, Termination Form, Reprimand, and Commendation could all be grouped into Human Resource Document. This refinement will happen in the design phase and will be strongly influenced by information gathered in the rest of the audit and by the overall strategy of the project. At this point, category assignments can be somewhat arbitrary and from the hip, reflecting current usage and understanding even if somewhat contradictory and redundant. Refinement will come in the design and implementation phases. One final piece of information you may want to capture is the *type* of the content in terms of format. Is it an image, video, audio, or text? The utility of this information will again be determined by the nature of the taxonomy project.

**Source** answers the question of from where the content came. This source usually takes the form of a tool such as Microsoft Word, Adobe Acrobat, Oracle Discoverer, and so forth. It may also take the form of an external provider such as the AP News Service, Lexus/Nexus or Greystone. What is important to capture is how the information is physically (or electronically) created. This will help with your IT assessment, let you know what resources you have as potential metadata sources as well as any technical constraints you must take into account. You may also want to capture any cyclic information available such as production cycle and schedule as an indicator of the contents volatility.

Once the content has been created and received, it is essential to track where it ends up. This is recorded under **Location**. With electronic content, this can be as straightforward as logging a URL or file system path. You must take care, however, to ensure that the content's location on the server or network is stable. If the content is archived periodically, you must note the archive schedule and the location of the archived files. The "Error 404" dead link syndrome, made famous by the World Wide Web, can render much of the audit useless if file movement patterns are not taken into account. The same applies to hard copy documents and physical content (CDs, DVDs, microfiche, etc.), except that there is rarely an established scheme for mapping physical locations. If file drawers and storage cabinets are already systematically labeled, take advantage of the scheme and associate your content with a location identifier (i.e., Room 12, File Cabinet 42, Drawer B). If such a scheme is not in place, create one prior to beginning the audit of hardcopy and physical materials.

As discussed above, a **Stakeholder** is anyone with a vested interest in the item of content being catalogued. Like content categories, stakeholders should be associated with a particular type. The primary stakeholder is generally the **author**. This is the individual or application responsible for the intellectual and informational content of the item. This may be separate and distinct from the **producer**, who is responsible for encapsulating that intellectual content in its current form. For example, a newsletter may have multiple *authors*, each contributing a column, but a single *producer*, the individual who formats the newsletter, slotting in the articles each author submitted. A **consumer** is anyone who makes use of the content; in this case a newsletter reader. The final basic stakeholder type is, oddly, a **stakeholder**. In this context, a *stakeholder* is an individual that does not directly contribute to the informational content of an item and does not directly use the content, but nevertheless has a vested interest in that content. In the newsletter example, this could be the head of the department issuing the newsletter. This person does not necessarily write articles, design the layout, or even read the newsletter in order to accomplish their job function, yet the newsletter represents their department and by association the executive.

Each stakeholder is associated with an **organization**. Generally, content itself is not directly associated with an organization. By creating the content-to-organization relationship by means of a stakeholder, you not only allow for multiple contexts and roles for each piece of content, you also have a point of contact for that content in each context. For example, a newsletter may be associated with the accounting office by means of its multiple *authors*, but is related to the public relations office by way of its *producer*. If you need clarification on informational content, you have the authors in accounting identified. If you need information on production and archiving cycles, you know that you must speak to the PR office. This is also useful in sorting out funding and budgets as well as ownership when project decisions must be made.

Finally, we come to the heart of the matter, the **terms** themselves. Starting with any terms suggested by the stakeholder interviews, begin to associate these words and even phrases with the content you are cataloging. Think of what terms are found within the content itself or that could be meaningfully inferred that would help in finding this content and determining its relevance to any given information need. This is distinct from the *location* discussed above. These terms are intended to help a user semantically associate content of which they were previously unaware with a question they are trying to answer. Some of this information can be drawn from the other elements in our content data model, but most of them will be drawn from the content itself. Limit yourself to five key terms per content item. This may be fleshed out in the design and implementation phase, but keeping the number limited will force you to focus on the critical aspect of the content and how it is used. It will also simplify the design process by eliminating extraneous terms in advance. Don't worry about losing critical information. If a term is essential to categorizing a document and all the other information in the model has been captured, it will be recommended by a stakeholder during analysis and review.

In addition to this brute-force, largely manual approach to content discovery, you can avail yourself of automation tools particularly when dealing with Web-based content. Most websites incorporate a search mechanism of some sort which will invariably generate a log of search terms attempted by users. By parsing these logs into a simple spreadsheet, sorting by frequency and again taking the top twenty percent, you can quickly generate a pool of candidate taxonomy terms that stakeholders are already using. Similarly, many tools such as Rational Rose and Microsoft Visio have the ability to automatically generate maps of websites and their content. Doing this in advance of the audit can help you formulate your plan of attack and also set some boundaries. At the very least, it will help you set realistic timelines for this phase of the project. Wherever possible, avail yourself of automatic data gathering tools. Unfortunately, true taxonomy work will always boil down to hands on, human driven consideration and labor. You will need a well thought out strategy to be successful.

# Creating a Governance Document

The central artifact of the research phase is the **governance document**. This document serves as the taxonomy bible. It goes beyond a project plan's timelines, milestones and deliverables. The governance document spells out what you are trying to accomplish, how you are going to get it done, who's going to do it and, most importantly, what you are not going to attempt. Clearly articulating the bounds of the project and documenting those boundaries is essential to keeping the taxonomy on track but also to determining whether you have succeeded or failed and to what degree. Your steering committee should take ownership of the creation and maintenance of the governance document. Calling the committee together for a strategy session to review the findings of the research phase (to date) and working through the basic elements of the governance document is a good approach. The full and final document will be fleshed out and vetted in subsequent sessions, but nothing beats locking the group in a room until a baseline plan is sketched out.

First on the agenda is a clearly articulated **statement of purpose**. In thirty words or less, you should be able to finish the phrase, "The main purpose of this taxonomy is..." Without the thirty-word restriction, these statements tend to ramble without focus. One sentence forces the group to pair the project down to its core intent. As a way of jumpstarting the process, or at least informing it, you may want to begin by completing the sentence, "The main objective (or concern) of the project's sponsor is..." Again in thirty words or less. Starting here will also make sure that everyone knows who is sponsoring the project (including the sponsor herself).

You will discover that it is surprisingly difficult to pin down what the enterprise wants to accomplish with a taxonomy. As an exercise, pose a series of goals to the group and have them rank them in importance. The following examples are fairly standard, but you should always adapt your proposed goals to the situation at hand.

- Easier/faster access to information resources
- Faster and greater responsiveness through informed decisions
- Increased collaboration
- Bridging different knowledge bases
- Elimination of manual indexing
- Establishing a corporate standard approach to information organization
- Decreased costs from information management (e.g., storage, paper, office space, etc.)
- Increased responsiveness/functionality to a known/targeted business application
- Lower costs for system support (e.g. training, development, etc.)
- Increased navigation/usability of corporate websites and/or corporate portals

Once you have come to a consensus on the ranking of your proposed goals, you should be able to amalgamate the top two or three into a succinct statement of purpose. As a reality check, determine how success in meeting those goals will be determined and measured. This needs to be a quantifiable determination, such as 50% reduction of status inquiry calls, 20% increase in page view times, or a 10% increase in revenue. Without pinning down a measurable way to determine success or failure, you will have a difficult time defending decisions made over the course of the project, especially if those decisions were compromises or reductions in scope. Once determined, these measures should be included in an "expected outcomes" section of the governance document.

Early in the document, you should also state who the audiences are and who the users and customers will be. You should have a fairly extensive list of candidates from the research phase (probably still underway at this point), but they now need to be formalized and often culled. To do this, list the top ten to twenty stakeholders identified so far and start grouping them into audiences. Make sure you attempt several different grouping strategies according to size of business unit, core function, revenue, geography, or whatever makes sense in the current context. Document the final groupings as your primary target audiences along with the criteria used to identify stakeholders and their assigned groups. Along with each group, list their primary needs and interests in the project. Try to think forward about how this is going to evolve over time and indicate, if not how this will be accommodated, at least that it will need to be addressed.

With the statement of purpose documented, along with how it maps to the intended audiences, the governance document should address what content is to be supported. This catalog needs to go beyond the basic content categories such as product literature, memo templates, and order forms. It also must go beyond formats such as Excel files, MPEG, PDF. This section must document how content revision will be addressed and whether or not versioning will be supported. You must also account for internal and external content and any dependencies these imply. Most importantly, what legacy content will be covered?

Along with the scope of content covered by the project, you must also determine how that content will be classified. The first decision to make is whether your approach will be top-down, bottom-up or a hybrid of the two. A top-down approach focuses primarily on the needs of the users and categorizes content accordingly. In this sense, it is a *prescriptive* approach that imposes an organizational structure on the content. A bottom-up approach is more *descriptive*, looking primarily at the content and identifying categories inherent in the collection itself, modifying and mapping these to the needs of the users as appropriate. In most cases, a bit of both styles will be required. State where each approach will be applied and how the two sets of results will be reconciled. Then drill down into each area and identify the rules that will be applied to develop categories and what rules will be used to assign content to those categories. If possible you should provide a business case to illustrate and justify these decisions.

The next section of the governance document should provide an overview of the taxonomy itself. This will not be the final structure, which will not emerge until well into the development phase, but should be the basic framework that will shape the taxonomy as it emerges. A simple taxonomy model can clearly demonstrate the structure you have selected, such as a strict hierarchical taxonomy, a faceted thesaurus or some other model. It will also help to clarify the organizational scheme that will be applied. This is an elaboration on content categorization but should be addressed in the taxonomy overview section as well.

These first four sections, Statement of Purpose, Supported Content, Content Classification, and Controlled Vocabulary Overview, represent the core of the governance document and the majority of your energies and those of your steering committee should be focused here. The remainder of the document should be fleshed out according to the situation of the current project. It may be useful to identify infrastructure-related matters such as network access rights, storage allocation, back-up and archiving facilities, mechanisms and responsibilities along with any standards that may impact these areas. If there is a content management system involved, a detailed analysis of how it will figure into the project and the long-term maintenance of the taxonomy is essential. As mentioned earlier, there should also be an "expected outcomes' section that details success criteria and measures.

Finally, there should be a signature page with a line for each member of the steering committee. The governance document is not complete and development cannot start until every member of that body has accepted the contents of the document and acknowledged ownership. Above all of the committee member signatures there should be a line for the sponsor. Once the steering committee has reached consensus and signed off, deliver the document to the sponsor. This should not be the first time she has seen it and nothing in the governance document should come as a surprise. Sign-off at this point should be a formality, but an important one. The sponsor's signature above those of the steering committee is your official sanction to carry out the project.

# 5

# Terms

The difference between the right word
and the almost-right word is the difference
between the lightning and the lightning-bug.

*Mark Twain*

The whole point of developing a taxonomy is to provide information producers and consumers with a common language for a particular area of knowledge. To do this, the vocabulary must be broad enough to describe the subject fully while staying succinct enough to be manageable. The key to finding this balance is **term selection**: selecting the right terms in the right form. Term selection is also the most difficult aspect of creating a taxonomy.

As you speak with stakeholders and peruse documents, you will start to understand what is important to the intended beneficiaries of the new taxonomy. You will encounter pet keywords, favorite search phrases and quirky filing systems. This will give you a feel for the local vernacular. All of these terms should be noted. By the time the content audit is complete and the governance document written, you will likely have amassed a few dozen **candidate terms** for the new taxonomy. These can serve as a good baseline as you move forward, but at this point it is time to fill in the gaps and start gathering terms in earnest.

When gathering terms, where you look and what you pick should be dictated by the scope of the taxonomy and its intended purpose. If your taxonomy will be used by several organizations, you will need to go beyond the walls of your own. If it will only be used to organize the Intranet page of a single department, it is probably not necessary to incorporate the complete Library of Congress Subject Headings. With each candidate term you must ask, "Does this fall within the scope of my subject, and will it be useful for the taxonomy's intended purposes?" When in doubt, always consult the governance document.

In general, term sources can be grouped as internal or external. **Internal sources** are those that are controlled by a single organization that is a stakeholder in the taxonomy. This could be the company that is paying for the taxonomy or a community of practice that will use the taxonomy, but has members spread across several companies. **External sources** are those that are relevant to the subject at hand, but do not have a vested interest in the taxonomy itself. This could include industry conventions, the product literature of suppliers or even competitors websites. Both internal and external sources must be taken into account when developing a pool of **candidate terms**.

# *Internal Term Sources*

You will have encountered most internal sources as you conducted a content audit. In particular you will have identified which documents and classes of document are most important to your audience. Your list will likely include invoices, purchase orders, compliance documentation, personnel action forms, meeting minutes, procedural documentation, and correspondence, among others. Each of these document classes should be revisited in light of the governance document and the increased understanding of the domain gained from the content audit. You will discover that there are critical documents your stakeholders failed to mention.

There are often entire classes of documents that are core to a business that stakeholders neglect because they themselves rarely refer to them. For example, an invaluable and yet often overlooked source of information is Standard Operating Procedure documents (SOPs). If these policy manuals exist, they can give you tremendous insights into how an area is supposed to run, even if the reality departs significantly from those policies. Often, attempts at term standardization have been made within these SOPs and can inform the structure of your taxonomy. They will also give you additional context and history for the project and environment.

Related to procedure documents and just as overlooked are orientation materials and "cheat sheets." Every organization will have materials to help new people get up to speed. These will reflect reality much more accurately than the official operation manuals. Cheat sheets translate corporate-speak into real language and document how work actually gets done rather than how its supposed to get done. While official language must be taken into account, so must its translation into daily parlance.

Day-to-day operations represent only a portion of the work done in an organization. A great deal of time and energy is devoted to projects, and these generate a lot of documentation. Scope documents, statements of work, project plans, team meeting minutes and status reports are a treasure trove of candidate terms and can provide insight into who has deep knowledge of specific areas in the company. As projects are staffed, those assigned to a given task will either have extensive knowledge in the pertinent areas or will develop it over the course of the project, making them **subject matter experts.** These individuals should be consulted to verify the validity of candidate terms and solicited for new candidate terms of their own.

It is unrealistic to read each and every collected document in depth. Fortunately, doing so is rarely necessary. Relevant terms can generally be identified from four areas: the document title, the table of contents, an executive summary, and chapter or section headings. Any of these may indicate that a particular area merits closer inspection, but most often accounting for these parts of the document will account for the whole.

As you collect and review these documents, it is important to consider where they live. Often this will be in a file folder on the organization's network. File systems, like the one pictured in the illustration, are interesting since their labels are rarely controlled. As a result, they reflect how the document owners think about them and how they can be located. This review will also expose abbreviations and acronyms that will need to be expanded and defined in the taxonomy. In this example, ASA, CFS, crc and DCH are all acronyms. ComRel is most likely an abbreviation, as is Anes. But what about CENSUS? It is entirely in capitals, which could indicate that it is an acronym or was a project title. It could also represent the concept of a census or an employee skill inventory. The point is that the file system itself is a reflection of how people interact with information resources within the organization, and as such it must be given due attention.

## *Intranets and Websites*

File systems and network drives are rapidly disappearing under the veneer of corporate Intranets. The intent of these networks of internal websites is to bring some order (or at least the appearance of order) to the free-for-all of the enterprise network. The links and labels presented on Intranets represent an ad-hoc attempt at term standardization,

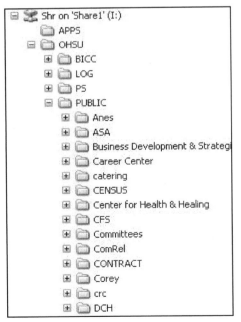

**Figure 1. A shared network file system.**

though too often it represents only the thoughts of the developer or administrator. The same holds true for external pages on the organization's website. This provides an opportunity to map internal terminology to external communications. Meaning and intent are often lost in translation between internal and external communications and messaging.

Similar to hardcopy document features, Web page titles, navigation buttons and pulldown menu options from both internal and external Web pages are excellent sources of candidate terms. In addition, the electronic medium offers capabilities not available from hardcopy. The most important of these arises from the near ubiquitous search box. The strengths and weaknesses of search have already been discussed, but the value of a search function in term gathering is undeniable. This is due to a simple fact. Whenever you search for information on the Web, you leave a trail.

Every interaction an information seeker has with a Web page is logged by the computer hosting that page. In addition to the date, time, origin and other vital statistics of the session, the server also records the query string used in the search that leads to the current page. Most search engines preserve a great deal more information about who is looking for what. **Search Analysis**, the process of examining these records, is perhaps the most powerful tool available for understanding how people look for information and what terms they associate with which concept.

Pictured in figure 2 is a report from a Web log analysis tool showing the top ten search phrases that lead Internet (external) users to a particular Web page over the course of ninety days. Below this is a report of Intranet user (internal) searches leading to the same page. Taken together, the reports offer a window into which terms information seekers are using to get to find your information. It also shows where the terminology of internal communications diverges from the language of customers, partners and others outside of the organization.

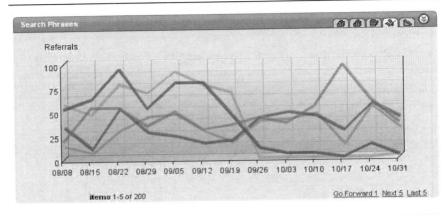

Figure 2. A web traffic report from WebTrends.

Of potentially even greater value are the search terms that result in no matching documents. If a certain word that does not match any documents crops up frequently in a search log, it is a strong indication that it is of high value to your users and it is not being accommodated. Terms like these deserve an asterisk in your list of candidate terms.

As discussed in Chapter One, findability issues often result from information seeker vocabulary not matching that of the information producer. Search logs, especially from Intranet search engines, can reveal the myriad different ways people ask for the same information. The table below shows that not only are official company holidays important to users, they have several different names for them. In addition to candidate terms, a search log entry of this sort sketches out a potential synonym ring. It also demonstrates spelling variants and mistakes, though some, like the last entry in the table, may remain in question.

| Search Phrase | Count |
|---|---|
| 2006 holidays | 43 |
| holiday policy | 28 |
| holiday leave | 21 |
| holiday schedule | 17 |
| 2007 holidays | 11 |
| holiday time off | 10 |
| holliday | 9 |
| 2006 holiday | 6 |
| holiday list | 6 |
| 2006 discretionary holiday | 4 |
| holiday calendar | 3 |
| corporate holiday | 3 |
| 2006 corporate holidays | 2 |
| 2006 holiday schedule | 2 |
| additional days off | 2 |
| additional holidays | 2 |
| holiday, additional | 2 |
| holiday lust | 1 |

# External Term Sources

Even if a taxonomy is intended for purely internal use, it is advisable to expand your search for candidate terms beyond strictly internal resources. Not doing so will leave your taxonomy vulnerable to ivory tower syndrome, in which the vocabulary is completely sensible and relevant to its creators alone and to no one else. The biggest culprit in this scenario is **term currency**. Terms and phrases can become so entrenched in an organization's culture that they remain in daily use even though the outside world has moved on. In addition, any domain will have a greater scope than what is currently in use by your organization. It is essential to at least be aware of what the subject looks like beyond the walls of your organization.

As with all things in the information age, the Internet is a good place to start. In addition to the obligatory Google search, subject portals should be consulted as a gateway to the current state of the field in any given subject. Portals, such as Intute, have a distinct advantage over general-public search tools. The resources they gather are selected by domain experts who deem them relevant and trustworthy. This effectively expands your pool of expertise at no cost.

Similarly, government portals, such as FirstGov.gov in the United States, provide access to both federal agencies and federally funded organizations. Terminology from these sources have several advantages. First is the breadth of coverage. As most governments have an agency for everything, chances are good that you will find a resource in the area your taxonomy is intended to cover. In most cases these resources will be presented in several different ways, by topic, organization or region as well as alphabetically, that can inform the structure your taxonomy eventually takes on. If the resource is a federally funded scientific or technical program, it will likely have been subject to peer review of some sort, which increases the quality and authority of the terminology. Finally, for better or worse, the vocabulary employed by these organizations as extensions of the federal government often become *de facto* standards for communication. This is especially true when regulation and compliance are involved. While they should not determine which terms you select for your taxonomy, consulting government resources can increase its applicability outside of your organization.

Beyond the Internet, traditional print media should also serve as a point of reference. Single subject encyclopedias and dictionaries provide in-depth information on any given topic and provide a good "fact check" for online sources. Bibliographic works, such as the ARBA Guide to Subject Encyclopedias and Dictionaries[1] are a good way to find out what is available. Journals and topic specific periodicals can verify the currency of terminology as well as provide additional domain expertise.

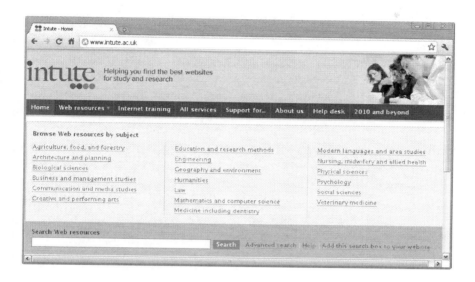

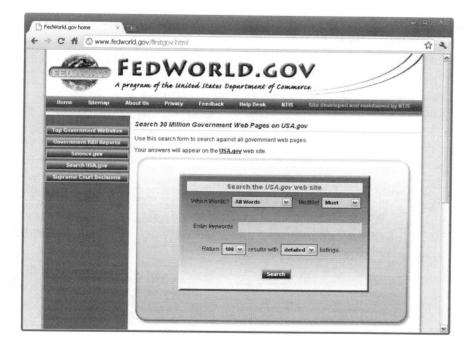

**Figure 3.  External portals as term sources.**

# *Existing Taxonomies*

A cardinal sin in information management is reinventing the wheel. This is especially true of creating taxonomies. While it is unlikely a controlled vocabulary already exists that is a perfect fit for your needs, there is most likely a taxonomy or thesaurus somewhere that overlaps your subject area. If you are working in the area of labor law, you should investigate both legal and labor vocabularies. Repositories, clearinghouses, and registries have started to emerge with significant coverage of available taxonomies. These vocabularies can often be licensed at a nominal cost and jump start your own development efforts.

| | |
|---|---|
| Taxonomy Warehouse | www.taxonomywarehouse.com |
| Controlled vocabularies, thesauri and classification systems available on the web | www.mpdl.mpg.de/staff/tkoch/publ/koslist.html |
| Controlling your language—links to metadata vocabularies | www.tasi.ac.uk/resources/vocabs.html |
| SWAD Europe thesaurus links | www.w3.org/2001/sw/Europe/reports/thes/thes_links.html |

As with any form of research, you have to know when to say "enough is enough." With the wealth of potential resources available, it is easy to become bogged down with slogging through every potential reference. This is unnecessary. The vast majority of your terms will come from internal sources. External resources should be used primarily to verify and inform the refinement of internal candidate terms and fill in the gaps. Once you have a pool of 100–500 terms that cover the subject, you should be ready to move on. This is a sufficient yet manageable number of candidate terms to start building the taxonomy.

# *Refining Terms*

The candidate terms collected thus far are the raw material of a taxonomy. As with any raw material, these must be refined before they are suitable for use. This involves basic hygiene, grammatical forms, disambiguation, factoring and selection of preferred terms. While not all of these processes will be applicable to every term, taken together they will ensure that the taxonomy as a whole consists of precise, unambiguous terms.

# *Basic Hygiene*

Spelling is the most fundamental refinement required for candidate terms. This goes beyond running spell check against the term list. As a rule of thumb, term spelling should conform to standard dictionaries such as Webster's and the Oxford English Dictionary, but there are exceptions. If a majority of your audience uses a variant spelling, one that differs from the dictionary spelling, the variant should be adopted. This is a user warrant in action, as discussed in Chapter Three. If there is more than one variant spelling in common use, they should all be retained and cross-referenced with each other. Additionally, a choice must be made as to what brand of English you will be using. Distinct differences exist between American English and British English, which can lead to ambiguity and confusion if not used consistently.

| **American English** | **British English** |
|---|---|
| col*or* | col*our* |
| dial*og* | dial*ogue* |
| che*ck* | che*que* |
| theat*er* | theat*re* |
| specialty | special*i*ty |

Consistency is also critical in how acronyms and abbreviations are handled. The fully expanded form of both should be used except in those cases where the acronym or abbreviation is more familiar. Most people are more comfortable saying DNA than deoxyribonucleic acid. They access their bank accounts from an ATM rather than an automated teller machine. Care must be taken to guard against ambiguity. Even though AI is easier to type than Artificial Intelligence, individuals looking for information on Artificial Insemination are likely to be disappointed.

To the extent possible, the use of special characters and punctuation should be avoided. Consider the name of a certain now defunct peer-to-peer network C*. Entering this into a search engine would be problematic since the asterisk is a near universal wildcard. Using C* as a search term would result in a match of every term beginning with the letter C. Ampersands have similar issues.

Another problem punctuation mark is the parentheses. Most search engines will interpret these as Boolean operators as in ((guns or butter) AND bread) vs. (guns or (butter AND bread)). Again, this can cause ambiguity. Parenthesis are often used to qualify a term as in English (American) or English (British), but these will usually become unnecessary as the taxonomy takes form as discussed later.

There are occasions where keeping punctuation is unavoidable. Hyphens are a common example. After all un-ionized particles are very different from unionized particles, and not acknowledging that fact could lead to subatomic labor disputes. Likewise apostrophes should only be retained as part of a proper name or to indicate a possessive case—or both as in O'Doul's Non-alcoholic Malt Beverage.

# Standards

In the realm of controlled vocabularies, two standards are the primary source of rules and recommendations for taxonomy construction and management: **ANSI Z39.19** and **ISO 2788**.

Z39.19, formally titled "Guidelines for the Construction, Format, and Management of Monolingual Controlled Vocabularies" is published and maintained by the **American National Standards Institute** or ANSI. This standard has evolved considerably since it first publication in 1974, which was focused primarily on printed resources and indexing collections of documents. Now in its fourth edition, Z39.19 provides guidance for the basic principles and concepts of controlled vocabularies in the context of online resources as well as traditional print media.

The standard is organized into eleven sections covering term selection and formatting, relationships, display and management. In addition, an eleven-page glossary of terms is provided along with an extensive bibliography that together provide a useful point of entry into the field.

The international companion to ANSI Z39.19 is ISO 2788 created and maintained by the **International Standards Organization**. It is much more succinct than the American standard, running only 32 pages versus the 172 of Z39.19, but covers roughly the same range of topics. Neither Z39.19 or 2788 address special issues, and they are intended as guidebooks for creating controlled vocabularies. To this end they provide clear examples for nearly every principle presented.

However, these principles are just that: principles rather than hard and fast rules. As Z39.19 itself states: "This standard should be regarded as a set of recommendations based on preferred techniques and procedures."

In most cases, the rules are presented in terms of "should" rather than "must."

> Each term included in a controlled vocabulary *should* represent a single concept.

> Hyphens generally *should not* be used in controlled vocabularies.

In many cases, the recommendations are even weaker, making certain elements and approaches completely optional.

> Diacritical marks *may* be used if they are required for proper names or by the accepted standards of the discipline.

> The generic nature of a relationship *may* be identified by the BT/NT coding.

Only rarely do the standards indicate mandatory rules.

> Apostrophes that are part of proper names *must* be retained.

Other requirements are raised by multilingual vocabularies. These are addressed separately in **ISO 5964**, "Guidelines for the establishment and development of multilingual thesauri."

Even in these cases the injunction to treat the standard as a "set of recommendations" remains. As a result there can be a wide variation in how taxonomies are structured and represented even when the standards are applied. This results largely from how taxonomies have traditionally been created.

Names deserve special attention while cleaning up candidate terms. First and foremost, you must decide whether or not to even include them in the taxonomy. In most cases, the right answer is to leave them out, including only those that are needed as access points to the vocabulary or that are desired as part of a hierarchy. For example, you may wish to include the Louvre, Getty and Guggenheim beneath the heading of Museums if doing so facilitates the aims of the taxonomy. Generally, names are best managed in a separate authority file that can be referenced or even linked with the taxonomy. This is especially true of proper names (does he go by William, Bill or Will?) Select as an entry term the name that is most familiar to the users of the taxonomy. Most people will look for U2's Bono rather than Paul David Hewson and Cher instead of Cheryl Sarkisian Lapiere. Having said this, it is important to retain an association with the less common name.

**Bono**
> UF Paul David Hewson

**Cher**
> UF Cheryl Sarkisian Lapiere

If you decide to include names in your taxonomy, it is important to put some guidelines in place. At a minimum, a standard should be identified to govern how names are to be handled. The most commonly used convention is currently the Anglo-American Cataloguing Rules, second edition (AACR2) published jointly by the American Library Association and the Canadian Library Association.

Each type of name has its own challenges. Consider the confusion possible from place names. People often uses the terms "England," "Britain," and "United Kingdom" interchangeably, but what do they actually mean? England is a single country. Britain or Great Britain is an island off the northwestern coast of mainland Europe encompassing England, Scotland, and Wales. The United Kingdom is actually made up of four countries and several territories, including England, Scotland, Wales, Northern Ireland, Bermuda, Gibraltar, Montserrat and Saint Helena among others. In casual conversation these distinctions may be unimportant but when calculating sales projections or population growth they are critical.

To address this potential ambiguity, a **scope note** should be applied. This is a brief explanation of the chosen meaning for a term as used in the taxonomy. In the example above, three scope notes should clear up any confusion.

> ### United Kingdom
> SN A political union made up of four constituent countries (England, Scotland, Wales and Northern Ireland) and including several overseas territories,
>
> ### Britain
> SN The island of Great Britain consisting of the of England, Scotland and Wales.
>
> ### England
> SN The largest and most populous country of the United Kingdom of Great Britain and Northern Ireland, occupying most of the southern two-thirds of the island of Great Britain

Familiarity also comes into play with place names. While it is best to use the official name of a place where possible, there are occasions when doing so is inappropriate. Very few people in the West would recognize North Korea by its official name: The Democratic People's Republic of Korea.

For most subject areas help is available in the form of authoritative references, many of which are available online. In the case of place names, the Getty Institute provides the Getty Thesaurus of Geographic Names (TGN).[3] Resources such as this can provide both official designations, common names and relationships to relevant organizations. Pictured in figure 4 is the Getty entry for England. For a broader range of subjects, the Library of Congress Authorities is hard to beat.[6]

The principle of most familiar term applies to most cases but there is not always a clear choice. Consider two religious organizations. It is very likely that the name "Quakers" is more recognizable than the official name, the "Religious Society of Friends," to most members of

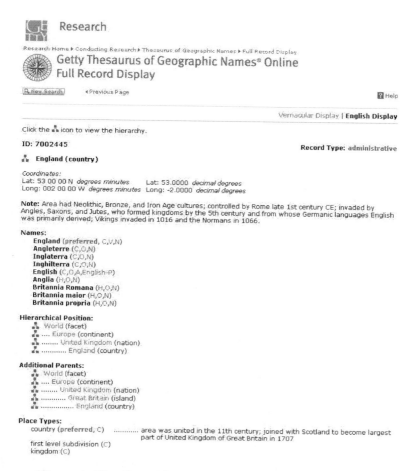

**Figure 4. The Getty Thesaurus of Geographic Names Online.**

the general public. But what about the "Mormons"? Recognition of this informal name is probably about equal with its official name "The Church of Jesus Christ of Latter-day Saints." In cases like this, the official name should be selected, again with the informal name associated.


Quaker
        UF Religious Society of Friends

Mormon
        USE Church of Jesus Christ of Latter-day Saints


What is most familiar often depends on the context of the taxonomy, most particularly its audience. Scientific names may most accurately represent a particular concept but may or may not be the best term choice depending on who will be searching for information. If a doctor is researching the effectiveness of a particular painkiller, "acetylsalicylic acid" would be an appropriate label. If an office worker is trying to relieve a headache, "aspirin" is more likely to come to mind. Trade names such as Tylenol, Coca-Cola or Post-Its can be tricky and generally should be treated as proper names as previously discussed. It is best to use a non-trade name as an entry term where possible. For example, "Transparent Tape" more accurately represents the concept than the more commonly used trade name "Scotch Tape." This practice can also help avoid some thorny trademark issues.

One final matter of basic term hygiene is the issue of plural versus singular. If the concept being represented can be counted—dogs, paperclips, airplanes, wind instruments—it should be plural. If it is difficult or impossible to count —dirt, wind, envy— it should be singular. A good rule of thumb for these more or less **concrete entities** is to group them as either objects (plural) or substances (singular). The exception to this is when a substance, say wine, has child terms, such as pinot noir, chardonnay, or Riesling, in which case the plural "wines" would be more appropriate. **Abstract concepts,** such as love, scholarship, line dancing, Brownian motion and the like, should be singular unless the term ends in an "s" or is normally pluralized as in "Mathematics" or "Logistics."

# *Compound and Precoordinated Terms*

Fledgling taxonomists tend to agonize over finding a single word that perfectly expresses a concept. While this is an admirable endeavor, it is often fruitless. Sometimes just one word is not enough to adequately express an idea. The concept of "North Carolina" would be difficult to reduce to a single term. This is an example of a **compound term**, or more formally a **lexime**: multiple words bound together as a single lexical unit. Multiword terms are perfectly acceptable in a taxonomy as long as certain rules are followed.

First and foremost it is important to distinguish between the idea of a compound term and a **precoordinated** term. Whereas a compound term uses multiple words to represent a single concept, a precoordinated term is the joining of two or more *concepts* in order to describe a narrower concept more precisely. For example, "New Hampshire" is a compound term describing a certain geographic area and population. "New Hampshire—Commercial Development— Permits and Forms" is a precoordinated term bringing together a state, an activity and a set of documents into a single category. Precoordinated terms are intended to help locate very specific information that is frequently accessed or to describe complex concepts that are commonly referenced within a certain subject.

Remember that information seekers will often combine terms to suit their immediate needs (postcoordinate retrieval). A searcher might enter the query "(New Hampshire AND Commercial Development AND (Forms OR Permits))." Combining them into a separate heading is a convenience to users and can dramatically simplify browsing and reduce the number of false hits in a search. This is especially true if the user is unfamiliar with the vocabulary or application. This convenience does come at a cost. Precoordinated terms will increase the size of the taxonomy and the cost of maintenance. Ultimately the determination of whether or not a complex precoordinated term is justified boils down to a user warrant. Consider the needs of your users. If a precoordinated heading will make their lives easier without making the taxonomy manager miserable, they are worth including (though sparingly).

Compound terms are more fundamental than precoordinated terms. Only a single concept is being represented, but more than one word is used. Each word in a compound term serves one of two functions. The **focus** represents the more general class of things represented by the whole, such as "Fiction" in "Science Fiction." The second term is a characteristic or attribute that distinguishes the term from the more general concept and is called the **difference** or **modifier**. In the case of "Science Fiction," "Science" is the modifier because we are representing a specific type of fiction. If "Fiction" were the modifier we would be talking about a specific sort of science.

It is important to know which word serves which purpose in order to determine if a compound term should be split up into single terms. Consider the difference between "Venetian Blinds" and "Blind Venetians." Sometimes the decision is obvious. Splitting terms like "Flying Buttresses", "Vocal Cords" or "Trade Winds" would result in ambiguity at best and nonsense at worst. In these examples, each word has a separate meaning unrelated to its role in the compound term. In other cases the compound term should be retained simply because of familiarity, as in "Gross Domestic Product."

In cases where the compound term is obviously the combination of multiple terms that can stand on their own, such as "Military Personnel" or "Brain Surgery" it should be split into individual terms. This form of **splitting**, or **syntactic factoring**, should also be done if the compound consists of an action and the thing performing the action, such as "Apple Picking" or "Bird Migration." If the focus is a property of something, as in "Bone Density" the term should be split.

A trickier form of splitting is **semantic factoring**, in which a term is broken down into separate terms based on its meaning. "Artificial

Pacemaker" could become "Cardiac" + "Regulation" + "Artificial" + "Implant." This can result in a single term actually being expanded into multiple, separate terms. For example, "Laryngitis" would be expanded to "Vocal Cords" + "Inflammation," and "Scoliosis" becomes "Spine" + "Curvature" + "Lateral." This may have advantages in certain classification situations, particularly in the medical or scientific realm, but semantic factoring often leads to the loss of the original term altogether. In general, it should be avoided.

# Grammatical Forms

No grammatical gymnastics are required when refining candidate terms. The form a term takes should remain as close to its conversational usage as possible. Nouns and noun phrases will represent the vast majority of terms in most vocabularies. Compound terms are usually adjectival noun phrases where the focus is the noun and the modifier is an adjective as in "Black Magic" or "Medicinal Herbs." When a compound is used, the normal word order should be retained. "Freudian Slips" should not become "Slips, Freudian."

As a general rule, adjectives do not appear as separate terms in a taxonomy. An exception to this may occur when the noun it is modifying is obvious from the context, such as a parent term in a hierarchy or when the term is an attribute of some object such as size ("Small," "Medium," "Large") or a color ("Red," "Green," "Blue"). The same holds true for adverbs. While they generally should not appear as free-standing terms, there are certain subjects where it makes sense. Music is one example where adverbs such as "Rubato," "Vivace," "Legato," or "Staccato" serve as stylistic indicators and can stand on their own in the taxonomy.

If the noun phrase contains a preposition such as "for" and "of," these should be omitted. "Veteran's Hospitals" is a better choice than "Hospitals for Veterans." Similarly, the definite article ("the") should be dropped as in "Arts" rather than "The Arts" and "Opera" instead of "The Opera." An exception to this rule is when the definite article is part of a proper noun or title, as in "The Big Lebowski." The same applies to initial articles in general, as in "A Lion in Winter" or "An Inconvenient Truth." Finally, if a verb is acting as a noun, the gerund is the best choice, as in "Reading" rather than "Read" or "Writing" instead of "Write."

# *Disambiguation*

We've discussed how to address synonyms, but what about **near synonyms** or **quasi-synonyms,** where the meaning of two terms is not exactly the same, but is pretty darn close? Technically "Salinity" is a different concept than "Saltiness" but is the distinction important enough to merit separate terms in the taxonomy? In most cases the answer is no, but again this must be driven by the vocabulary's domain, purpose and audience. Generally, the term that most broadly encompasses the concept and is most familiar to users should be selected.

This addresses the issue of having too many terms for a single concept. The opposite situation, **polysemy**, where one term can refer to more than one concept is more difficult. Does "Bank" refer to a financial institution, the edge of a river, a slope, or the cushion of a billiard table? **Disambiguation** is the process of clarifying which concept is intended when several are possible.

Where possible compound terms should be used to clarify which meaning is intended for a particular term. However, with homonyms like "Bank," or "Fair" (appearance), "Fair" (exhibition), and "Fair" (reasonable) a compound term isn't always practical. One approach is to simply define the term in a scope note. While full dictionary descriptions are generally too verbose for this purpose, a brief definition can be added to the term to explain its intended use. If there is a near-synonym that will be included in the taxonomy, or two distinct terms which may be confused such as "Eczema" and "Psoriasis," **reciprocal scope notes** should draw attention to the distinction.

### Eczema

SN    A non-contagious inflammation of the skin, caused by environmental irritants or allergies, characterized chiefly by redness, itching, and the outbreak of lesions that may become encrusted and scaly. Distinguished from **Psoriasis**, which is an autoimmune skin disease with a strong genetic component.

### Psoriasis

SN    An autoimmune skin disease with a strong genetic component characterized by inflammation of the skin appearing as reddened, rough, raised, and slightly itchy skin covered with silvery, scaly flakes. Distinguished from **Eczema**, which is caused by environmental irritants or allergies.

There are two problems with the scope note solution to ambiguity. It requires users of the taxonomy to actually read the definition, and it forces the taxonomy team to agree on a definition. A simpler approach that may be used in lieu of or in conjunction with scope notes are **qualifiers**.

A qualifier is simply an additional term added to the main term to distinguish between homonyms. This is different from a compound term in that while the additional word is considered part of the term itself, it is set apart by punctuation, usually parenthesis. This is especially useful if the taxonomy covers a multidisciplinary domain.

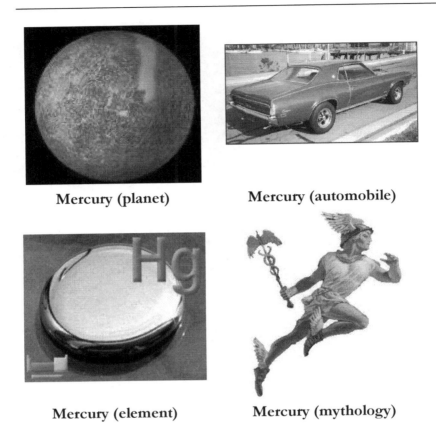

Mercury (planet)          Mercury (automobile)

Mercury (element)         Mercury (mythology)

**Figure 5. Using qualifiers to disambiguate terms.**

Where possible, a compound phrase should be used rather than a single-word term with a qualifier, as in "Civil Rights" rather than "Rights (civil)". When qualifiers are necessary, they must be standardized across the taxonomy. A single term should be selected to indicate a particular domain. For example, either biosciences or biology is an appropriate qualifier but it must be one or the other, not both.

Binder              (Biology)
Clamping            (Biology)
Linkers             (Biology)

- or -

Binder              (Biosciences)
Clamping            (Biosciences)
Linkers             (Biosciences)

- not -

Binder              (Biology)
Clamping            (Lifesciences)
Linkers             (Biosciences)

While the comprehensiveness and quality of a pool of terms is essential to the success of any taxonomy, it is not sufficient. The structure of the taxonomy is critical and deserves at least as much attention as refining the terms it will organize. A well designed hierarchy, network, or matrix can do as much to distinguish terms as any number of qualifiers and scope notes. Once you have amassed, cleaned, and formatted between 100 and 500 candidate terms, you are ready to start organizing them into the final structure of the taxonomy. Structure, as discussed in the next chapter, can also eliminate ambiguity.

# 6

# Structure

It turns out that an eerie type of chaos
can lurk just behind a façade of order
and yet, deep inside the chaos lurks
an even eerier type of order.
                            —Douglas Hofstadter

Staring down a large pile of unorganized, candidate terms can be daunting. When faced with the prospect of marshalling all of these words into some as yet undefined structure that will satisfy every stakeholder, you may be tempted to just sort them alphabetically and declare victory. After all, just going through the process of collecting and cleaning the terms has put you ahead of the game. You now have a reasonable understanding of what information is used in your organization, how it is used, and by whom. You have documented the terminology used by members of the community to interact with that information and with each other. Isn't providing a simple list of those terms sufficient?

Unfortunately, the answer is no. As anyone who has traveled can tell you, words aren't language. An American alone in China will not get very far armed with just a list of Mandarin words. You must know how each of those words translates to your native tongue and how to string them together in a way that makes sense to the locals. You also need to be able to do this quickly so that the person you are attempting to communicate with doesn't get bored and walk away as you frantically flip through your phrase book. Your vocabulary needs structure.

In order to be useful, the structure of a taxonomy cannot be completely artificial. Just as the terms themselves were discovered within the content and the community of the domain, the structure should also emerge from the raw materials. Occasionally, this structure will emerge of its own accord. Usually, however, it must be dragged kicking and screaming out of your pool of candidate terms. This process requires breaking the list down into manageable chunks and shuffling the pieces until they start coalescing into sensible groups. Card sorting will get you started.

## *Card Sorting*

**Card sorting** has been used as a technique for discovering how to structure and organize information for over a decade. Information architecture gurus Lou Rosenfeld and Peter Morville have called card sorting one of "the most powerful information architecture research tools in the world…and can provide insight into users' mental models, illuminating the ways they often tacitly group, sort and label tasks and content within their own heads."[1] What cutting edge technologies are required to take advantage of this powerful technique? 3" x 5" cards and a pen.

A card sort asks users to take candidate terms and group them in whatever way they think makes sense. That's basically all there is to it. The power of this simple technique lies in the thought patterns and information habits it reveals. A rough taxonomic structure will begin to emerge as participants sort and shuffle terms according to how they would look for information or accomplish a task.

To prepare for conducting a card sort, label index cards with each of the candidate terms, one term per card (see figure 1). On the reverse side of the card write an identifier that will help you track where a

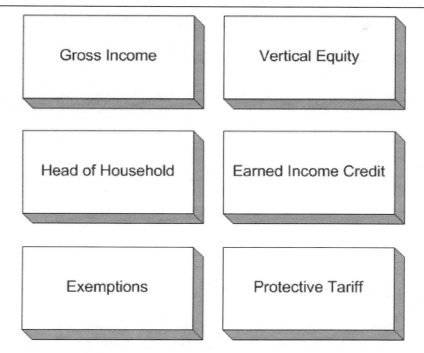

**Figure 1. Candidate terms in a simple card sort.**

particular term gets placed. In most cases simply numbering the cards will do. It is important to not have the identifier visible on the same side of the card as the candidate term itself, as this may influence how the participant groups the terms (see figure 2). If there is a chance that the term may be misinterpreted, include a brief definition or even an image below the identifier.

Participants should be drawn from every group that has an interest in the taxonomy being developed. It is best to have more than one representative from each group, as this increases the odds of the sort being representative of that group's interests as a whole. You may have the participants perform the sort individually or in teams, though teams should be limited to three or at most four members.

Team sorts tend to be more interesting, as team members will usually discuss and debate where any given term belongs. These interactions should be encouraged and captured as it will provide a richer picture

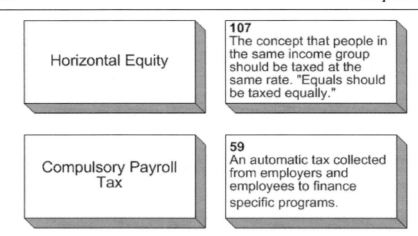

**Figure 2.  Card sorts with identifiers and definitions.**

of how information is used in the organization. Even with individual sorts, this type of information may be captured by encouraging the participant to "think aloud" or by asking why they placed a certain term where they did, though you must be careful not to challenge a grouping or influence their decisions.

There are no rules governing how terms are to be sorted. Each participant or team should group terms as they see fit. Sub-grouping is fine. A "miscellaneous" bucket is fine. A "I really don't care about this topic" group is allowable and can actually be useful in weeding out irrelevant content. You should also have a stack of blank cards available on which participants can add terms or duplicate an existing term if they feel it needs to be in more than one category. Encourage them to ask questions and experiment. A term can be moved from group to group as often as necessary. Groups can be created and eliminated at whim. The goal is not to get it right the first time, but to get it to make sense to the person doing the sort.

The number of cards used can be tricky. Too many and participants will feel overwhelmed and either give up or begin to group terms carelessly or even randomly just to be finished. Too few cards and the structure will not be representative of the entire vocabulary. The appropriate number of cards depends on the nature of the application and the scope of the vocabulary itself. For a small taxonomy, 30–40 cards will often be sufficient. For a more complex domain, closer to 100 should be used. More than 100 cards may tax participant's energy level and patience. This is a problem if you have 500 candidate terms. If this is the case, select 100 terms that seem to represent the entire domain. Keep this set of cards constant across every individual or group that performs the card sort. Divide the remainder of the cards evenly across each group. For example, if you have a total of 460 terms to be sorted and five different groups that will perform a sort, each group will receive the basic set of 100 words plus 72 of the remaining terms ($460 - 100 = 360 / 5 = 72$). 172 cards is manageable, and the entire candidate pool will still be sorted.

Once the participant is comfortable with how they have grouped the terms, ask them to label each group. This can be more difficult than it would seem. While performing the sort, participants will group terms intuitively. Asking them to label their groups will force them to validate their intuition and provide further insights into their mental model of the information being organized.

With all terms grouped and each group labeled, the card sort is complete. Because it was conducted with no preconceptions or limitations it is considered an **open card sort**. A variation on this approach is the **closed card sort** in which categories are predefined and participants are asked to sort terms into these existing groups. Open card sorts are useful in discovering structure. Closed card sorts are ideal for validating that structure.

Once the sort is complete, the results should be loaded into a spreadsheet and analyzed. Record each category that was defined during the sorts and a count of each time a term was assigned to each category. Patterns will quickly begin to emerge. If a particular term was assigned to the same category a high percentage of the time, that is probably where it belongs in the final taxonomy. If a particular group has an unwieldy number of terms or conversely only a couple of terms assigned to it, the category needs to be refined.

Analyzing the results of a card sorting exercise can be as simple as "eye-balling" the piles of cards on the table or as sophisticated as a complete statistical analysis. The depth of the analysis depends on the scope of the vocabulary and the complexity of the application. Card sort software tools such as XSort and SynCaps provide **cluster analysis** and graphic representations such as **denograms** and **surface maps** that can reveal patterns that would otherwise be missed. Card sort tools can also be useful in managing large card sorts across multiple sessions. Based on the patterns that are revealed by your analysis, the various card sorts should be reconciled into draft categories. Once this is done, synonyms can be addressed. During the card sort, synonyms should naturally gravitate into the same groupings. Sort each group alphabetically and move synonyms to the same line of your spreadsheet. Select the preferred term from among the options for each entry.

**claims**

       appeal
       casualty
       commission
       injury
       loss
       property damage
       stipend
       theft

**claims**

       appeal
       casualty, loss, injury, property damage, theft
       commission
       deficit
       stipend

**casualty**      USE FOR loss, injury, property damage, theft
       loss USE casualty
       injury USE casualty
       property damage USE casualty
       theft USE casualty`

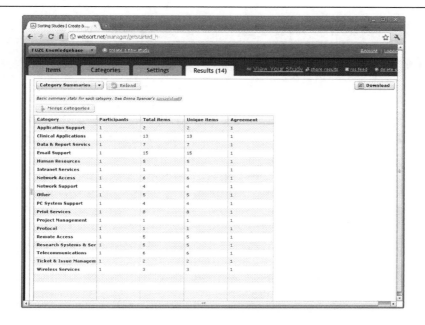

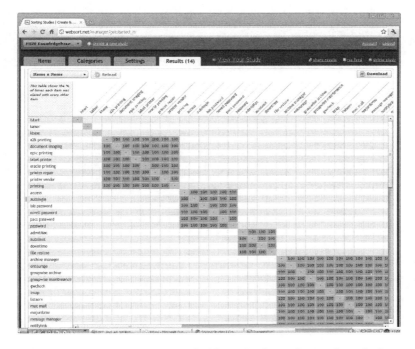

**Figure 3. Tools like websort facilitate both sorting and analysis .**

## Categories and Facets

Reconciling the card sorts of different stakeholders will give you a good idea of what is going on in the heads of your users, but it will not necessarily yield a usable structure. People will group content according to their own mental model of the domain. Those models do not always reflect reality and even if they do, reality can sometimes be improved.

The first step is to verify that all of the terms assigned to a particular category represent the same type of concept. If the category is mostly comprised of "things" then it should only contain "things." Similarly, if a category groups together processes and actions then those are the only sort of concept it should contain. This can be subtle. Consider the term "Anatomy," which can refer to either a collection of things, i.e., body parts, or a discipline, i.e., the study of that collection of body parts. The sense in which the word "Anatomy" is used in the taxonomy will determine how it should be related to other terms. If it refers to the structure and makeup of an organism, then the parts of that organism, heart, lungs, etc., would fall naturally under the "Anatomy" category.

```
anatomy
        respiratory system
                upper respiratory system
                        epiglottis
                        larynx
                        esophagus
                lower respiratory system
                        bronchi
                        lungs
                        diaphragm
```

If it is used to refer to the discipline, then things like the respiratory system, a part of the body that can be studied within the discipline of anatomy, would not fit. Instead the Anatomy category would contain the subdisciplines of the field.

```
anatomy
        anatomic pathology
        cell biology
        embryology
        gross anatomy
        histology
        neuroanatomy
        radiologic anatomy
```

The defining characteristic of a category is its **principle of division**. There are no fundamental characteristics that are applicable to every taxonomy. What constitutes an appropriate defining characteristic will vary from category to category and from taxonomy to taxonomy. Consistency within a category is the critical factor.

As the categories begin to take shape it will become apparent that they are of different sorts. Some may collect processes and actions, others will organize objects by name and still others may be grouped by role, situation, or even physical characteristics. If these categories can be made orthogonal to each other, that is mutually exclusive, then a faceted structure is possible and usually desirable. As discussed in Chapter Three, faceted classification offers several advantages over strictly hierarchical taxonomies. Faceted taxonomies are extremely flexible and expressive and are able to describe a single object or concept from multiple perspectives. Their flexibility also allows them to easily incorporate new concepts, even after the vocabulary has been created and placed in service.

Selecting appropriate facets is as tricky as it is essential. Ranganathan, Father of Facets, tried to provide clear instructions regarding how to go about this. To do so, he codified his theories of faceted classification in a system of canons (rules that must be followed), postulates and principles (very strong suggestions). Unfortunately, his complete system consists of 46 canons, 13 postulates and 22 principles. This is enough to intimidate even the most intrepid library scientist, not to mention information architects.

To address this, one of those intrepid library scientists, Dr. Louise Spiteri of Dalhousie University, has developed a simplified version of Ranganathan's system.[2] Spiteri offers seven guiding principles for selecting facets.

- **Differentiation**: When dividing an entity into its component parts, it is important to use characteristics of division (i.e., facets) that will distinguish clearly among these component parts.

- **Relevance**: When choosing facets by which to divide entities, it is important to make sure that the facets reflect the purpose, subject, and scope of the classification system.

- **Ascertainability**: It is important to choose facets that are definite and that can be ascertained.

- **Permanence**: Facets used in a classification system should continue to be used as long as there is no change in the purpose of the system.

- **Homogeneity**: Facets must be homogeneous.

- **Mutual Exclusivity**: All the facets used to divide an entity must be mutually exclusive, i.e., no two facets can overlap in content.

- **Fundamental Categories**: There exist no categories that are fundamental to all subjects… [C]ategories should be derived based upon the nature of the subject being classified… Identify fundamental categories by reference to the context of the subject itself… [N]o one list of fundamental categories should be imposed mechanically upon subjects … [N]o one list may be necessarily exhaustive or applicable to all subjects.

While Ranganathan's classic five facets (Personality, Matter, Energy, Space, Time) are still excellent starting points, the range of potential facets goes far beyond PMEST. The United Kingdom's Classification Research Group (CRG) recognized this in the early 1970s and developed a new approach to faceted classification that extends Ranganathan's rubric to include thirteen basic categories.

- thing/entity
- kind
- part
- property
- material
- process
- operation
- patient
- product
- by-product
- agent
- space
- time

The comprehensiveness of this list is borne out by its role in the creation and maintenance of the second edition of the Bliss Classification system (BC2). BC2 is the classification standard for British Libraries and Information Centers. It currently consists of sixteen published volumes all organized around the thirteen facets defined by the CRG.

Despite the all-inclusive nature of the BC2 facets, they may not meet the needs of a specific vocabulary. Vanda Broughton, one of the joint editors of BC2, has said, "These fundamental thirteen categories have been found to be sufficient for the analysis of vocabulary in almost all areas on knowledge. It is however quite likely that other general categories exist."[3] Classification systems like BC2 and others should be used as references and starting points. Ultimately, the choice of facets comes down to what is appropriate for the domain and the intended use of the vocabulary. For example, the culinary website epicurious.com is organized around food and cookery facets targeted at a non-specialist audience.

- course
- cuisine
- season/occasion
- type of dish
- preparation method
- source
- main ingredients

The groups created in the card sorts will give a strong indication of what facets are needed and even if facets are appropriate.

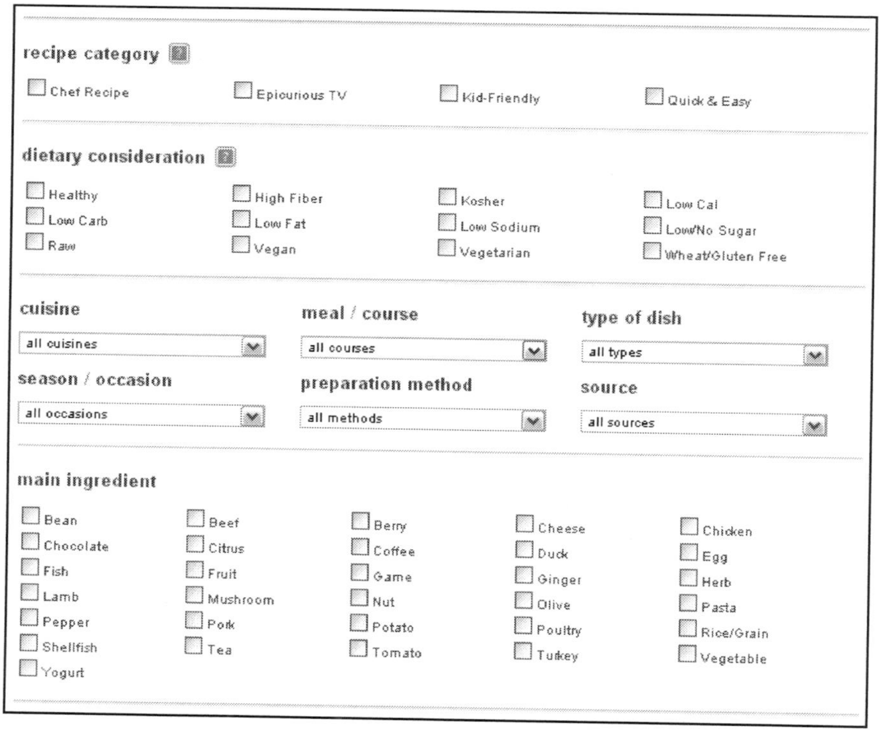

**Figure 4. Search facets from the website epicurious.com.**

# *Relationships*

Sorting terms into consistent groups or facets accomplishes more than simply creating manageable piles of words. It begins to define the relationships among those words. It is important to decide what the nature of these relationships are to be within each category as the overall structure of the taxonomy will emerge from those choices. Just as an explicit principle of division will help to ensure consistent categories, defining the type of relationship used in each category will help create a usable and sustainable architecture for the vocabulary.

The simplest type of relationship declares that something is a member of a particular category or class as a **broader** or **narrower** term. Usually the term is a more specific member of a class. For example, a "femur" is a more specific type of bone. This type of link is a **generic relationship**, or more simply an **IsA relationship**. This is the most fundamental hierarchical relationship.

**bone**
      NT femur
      NT fibula
      NT tibia

**femur**
      BT bone

**fibula**
      BT bone

As simple as they may first appear, generic relationships should not be taken for granted. In order to be valid, every instance of the narrower term must be an instance of the broader term. Conversely, only some instances of the broader term can accurately be labeled with the narrower term. For example, *all* mushrooms are fungi, but only *some* fungi are mushrooms, so this is an appropriate generic

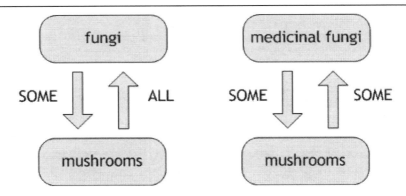

**Figure 5.   Generic hierarchical relationships must pass the ALL/SOME test to be valid.**

relationship. On the other hand, if you make the broader term more specific, say "medicinal fungi," the relationship breaks down. Some medicinal fungi are in fact mushrooms, but not all mushrooms are medicinal.

Another form of the IsA relationship occurs when a term represents a particular instance of its category. North America is an instance of a continent. The United States is an instance of a country, Pennsylvania is an instance of a state and so forth.

        (Continents)
           Africa
           Asia
           Europe
           North America

               (Countries)
                  Canada
                  Mexico
                  United States of America

                       (States)
                           Alabama
                           Alaska
                           Arizona
                           Arkansas

A category can also be organized as a hierarchy of parts when each broader term represents the whole. This creates a natural hierarchy.

```
airplane
          fuselage
          wing
                    aileron
                    flaps
                    rudder
                    spoiler

circulatory system
          heart
                    aorta
                    atrium
                    pulmonary artery
```

This **whole-part relationship** can get tricky when a term can be a part of several different things. A "rudder" can be a part of a boat as well as an airplane. Often this will result from increasing the specificity of a category. If the category "circulatory system" is sub-divided into "coronary circulatory system" and "pulmonary circulatory system" there will be two equally valid slots for "heart." In some cases this represents a true polyhierarchy in which the term in question truly belongs in more than one category. For example, neurology and pharmacology are separate and distinct disciplines within the life sciences. Neurology is the science of the nervous system. Pharmacology studies drugs. The field of neuropharmacology studies the effect of drugs on the nervous system. Neither parent term, neurology or pharmacology, completely encompasses the more specific field of neuropharmacology. It is a part of both parent terms, so both relationships should be captured.

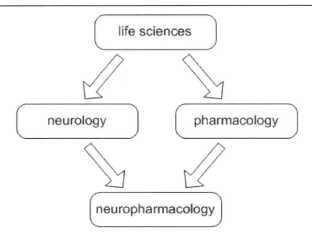

**Figure 6. A whole-part relationship polyhierarchy**

Polyhierarchies can also occur in generic or IsA relationships. A piano has all the properties of both a string instrument and a percussion instrument and so may be properly placed in both categories.

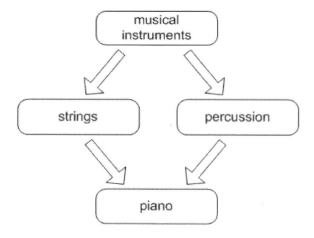

**Figure 7. A generic relationship polyhierarchy.**

Polyhierarchies are also referred to as **entangled vocabularies** and should be used sparingly as they can get very messy. Consider the parts of an airplane mentioned earlier. If we start creating polyhierarchies by including the rudder as both an airplane part and a part of a sea vessel we have opened a large can of worms. What do we do with the "wing"? It can be a part of an airplane, a bird, a building, a chair, a stage, or even a faction within a political party. If all of these associations are captured in a hierarchical, parent-child or whole-part manner, the structure of the vocabulary can quickly disintegrate into an unmanageable web. Despite this fact, it is not necessary to lose the relationships among terms with multiple parent terms.

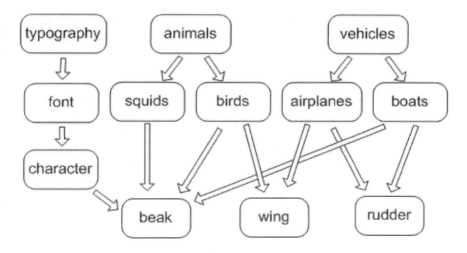

**Figure 8. Polyhierarchies can quickly get out of control.**

If a definitive parent-child relationship (whole-part, instance or generic) cannot be identified between two terms, the link between them may still be important enough that it should be made explicit in the taxonomy. These should be captured in **associative relationships**. For example, contact lenses and glaucoma are definitely relevant to the subject of eyes, but don't fit cleanly into any of the standard hierarchical relationships. Nevertheless, the association should be captured with as a **related term**.


**eye**
> cornea
> iris
> lens
>
> RT glaucoma
> RT cataract


Generally, associative relationships are used to link terms that exist in separate subjects or hierarchies. In certain situations, they can prove useful in guiding an information seeker between terms within a single hierarchy. The most common reason for using an associative relationship within a single hierarchy is an overlap in meaning between two terms, but that are not actual synonyms such as boat and ship, hotel and motel, or tavern and saloon. Derivational relationships within a single hierarchy may also be represented by a related term association. For example, horses, donkeys and mules are all more specific instances of equines, but the additional information that a mule is the product of a mule and a horse should also be captured.

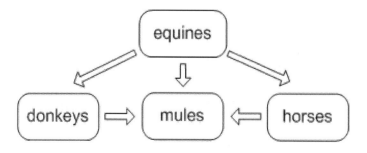

**Figure 9. A derivational relationship in a single hierarchy**

**equines**
    donkeys
        RT horses
        RT mules
    horses
        RT donkeys
        RT mules
    mules
        RT donkeys
        RT horses

Associative relationships do not necessarily need to be reciprocal. It is perfectly valid to include one-way or **asymmetric relationships** in the vocabulary if it serves an information finding need. A person exploring the topic of "population control" would likely find relevant information under the topic of "family planning." It is less likely that someone browsing contraceptive options under the heading of family planning would be interested in global birth-rate trends. As a result, only one of the associative relationships needs to be captured.

**population control**
    RT family planning

**family planning**
    abstinence
    contraception
    reproductive health

It is very easy to insert a bias into the viewpoint of the vocabulary by including or omitting certain associations. This is fine as long as it is intentional, acknowledged, and serves the stated purpose of the vocabulary. Associative relationships can be a great aid to an information seeker by suggesting associations they might not think of in a particular context. They should, however, be restricted to the periphery of the subject. The core concepts and elements of any

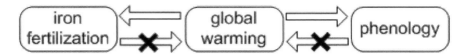

**Figure 10. Associative relationships, especially asymmetric ones, should be kept at the margins of a subject.**

given category should be integral to its basic structure in order to provide adequate context and coverage. This will also help reinforce the structure of the overall vocabulary.

Once the relationships among terms within each category are established, you must organize the categories themselves into an overall structure for the taxonomy. This largely boils down to determining the order of categories in the taxonomy. The same guidelines for order of terms within a category still apply: general before specific, and abstract before concrete. Other situation-specific approaches to ordering, such as chronological or geographical, may also be used as the application warrants.

Finalizing the categories and facets completes the taxonomy (as far as any taxonomy can ever be considered "complete"). Unfortunately, there is still work to be done if it is not to become an island unto itself. As taxonomies find their way into more and more applications and are applied across an enterprise, it becomes increasingly important to represent them in a manner that facilitates interoperability. Just exchanging spreadsheets of terms via email is no longer sufficient.

# 7

# Interoperability

I would not give a fig for the simplicity
this side of complexity,
but I would give my life for the simplicity
on the other side of complexity.

Oliver Wendell Holmes

Despite the explosion of the taxonomy software and services industry over the past several years (it has been growing at an average annual rate of 21% since 2002), the vast majority of taxonomies are still created and maintained in Microsoft Excel. Spreadsheets are easy to create and nearly everyone has a copy of Excel, so sharing a taxonomy with colleagues is simple. But while shuffling terms from column to column may come as second nature to even a novice taxonomist, problems arise once the taxonomy is complete and ready to be used. Once you have created a taxonomy, the question is how do you move that taxonomy around? How do you have it in one system and export it to another system?

Most will answer this question by exporting the vocabulary to a simple comma-delimited file. This approach worked just fine when it was only people using the taxonomy with maybe one application that actually needed to ingest it. Things are not that simple anymore. Most enterprise infrastructures now consist of multiple applications that must interact and need to understand a common vocabulary to do so. Unfortunately, each one of those systems will have its own way of looking at a comma-delimited taxonomy file. A content management system may look at the word in the second column as a child of the term in the first column of the same row while your search engine looks at the row above for that relationship. The categorization engine may not even look for terms until it gets to the fourth or fifth column of the file. The taxonomy must be shared in a way that retains the role or function of each term in relation to the entire vocabulary. To accomplish this a structured format is needed. Currently, the best option is the **eXtensible Markup Language (XML)**.

```xml
<vocabulary>
   <vocabulary_name>wines</vocabulary_name>
   <vocabulary_id>00462</vocabulary_id>
      <facet>
       <facet_name>wine type</facet_name>
       <facet_id>WDC3092</facet_id>
       <term>Red Wines</term>
       <term> White Wines</term>
       <term>Bubbly</term>
       <term>Sherry</term>
       <term>Port</term>
      </facet>
</vocabulary>
```

**Figure 1.  A taxonomy fragment with basic XML tags.**

# *Basic XML Concepts*

As its name indicates, XML is a markup language meaning that it adds information to a document, usually in the form of <tags> </tags>, breaking it up into well defined components or **elements**. These elements allow you to explicitly indicate the role and function of a piece of text or data. The characteristics of a particular element can be captured as attributes. For example, a term in a taxonomy could be represented as

<node name="Abdominal Pain" id="T3061" parent="G31">

Here, <node> encapsulates the term itself as a structural unit in the taxonomy. The attributes name, id, and parent describe the key characteristics of the term, including its label "Abdominal Pain," how it is uniquely identified within the vocabulary "T3061" and relates it to the next broader term in the hierarchy "G31."

The "extensible" in eXtensible Markup Language ensures that you can define the exact structure you need for the task at hand and communicate it clearly. The above example could also be represented as

<term id="T3061" parentId="G31">Abdominal Pain</term>

How the various elements of a document come together to represent its structure is defined and documented in a **document type definition (DTD)** or **schema** (figure 2). The schema serves as a set of rules or a grammar for creating a particular type of document, in our case a taxonomy. By tying a document to a particular **schema** or DTD, it becomes possible to automatically verify that it conforms to the rules governing that type of document. This is done with a **document type declaration**.

```
<?xml version="1.0" encoding="UTF-8"?>
<!DOCTYPE taxonomy SYSTEM "E:/simple_taxo.dtd">
```

This is critical to interoperability. In order to be easily understood by a computer or application, a taxonomy must be both **well formed**, conforming to all the rules of XML, and **valid**, organized according to the grammar specified in the DTD.

```
<?xml version="1.0" encoding="UTF-8"?>
<!ELEMENT taxonomy (term+)>
<!ELEMENT term (synonym*, property*,term*, child*)>
<!ATTLIST term
          Name          CDATA          #REQUIRED
          id            CDATA          #IMPLIED
          parent        CDATA          #IMPLIED
>
<!ELEMENT child EMPTY>
<!ATTLIST child
          id            CDATA          #REQUIRED
>
<!ELEMENT synonym EMPTY>
<!ATTLIST synonym
          name          CDATA          #REQUIRED
>
<!ELEMENT property (#PCDATA)>
<!ATTLIST property
          name          CDATA          #REQUIRED
>
```

**Figure 2. A simple DTD.**

Related to the document type declaration is the notion of an XML **namespace**. If a document contains an element tagged as <table>, it would be useful to know where that element is defined. A schema defined by a database engineer would probably define a table very differently than would a carpenter's DTD. A namespace indicates where a particular XML element is defined by adding a prefix and an identifying name to an element. For example:

```
<taxo:term xmlns:taxo="http://www.taxo_example.org">
```

specifies that the element "term" is taken from a namespace named "http://www.taxo_example.org." This prevents confusion with other possible definitions of "term" that may find their way into an application, such as term of office:

```
<politics:term xmlns:politics="http://www.politics.gov">
```

The URLs (actually URIs, Uniform Resource Identifiers) used in namespaces are just unique identifiers. An application using the document does not generally look up any information at the location specified. Often, however, namespace URIs do point to a real Web page containing information about the namespace.

Namespaces are particularly handy in defining vocabulary structure as they allow you to mix and match existing document types. Consider the problem of combining multiple taxonomies into a single-faceted vocabulary. If useful element definitions exist in the schemas of the source vocabularies, it may seem simpler to combine them into a single new schema. Beyond difficulties of ownership and maintenance, this often leads to conflicting element definitions. In one file, terms might be represented as <term>butter</term>, in another as <term id=1634 name="butter" parent =635>, and in the faceted taxonomy schema as <term facet_id = 5 label="butter">. Which is the correct representation for the new combined vocabulary? A better approach is to define namespaces for each source schema and assign prefixes within the new vocabulary.[1]

```
<taxo:taxonomy
    xmlns:taxo="http://www.taxo_example.org"
    xmlns:fac="http://www.facet_example.org">
        <taxo: vocabulary>
            <fac: facet name="color">
                    <taxo:term>red</taxo:term>
                    <taxo:term>blue</taxo:term>
                    <taxo:term>green</taxo:term>
            </fac:facet>
        </taxo: vocabulary>
</taxo:taxonomy>
```

# *Representing Hierarchy*

XML is hierarchical by nature. A DTD or schema defines a single root node from which all other elements branch in neat parent/child relationships. As an application processes an XML encoded document, the content is parsed into this tree structure. As a result, XML maps very naturally to the hierarchies inherent in taxonomies. The extensible nature of XML allows for multiple ways of representing hierarchy, each with its own strengths and weaknesses. The most direct approach is to simply embed the hierarchy directly in the list of terms.

```
<term name="color" id=1>
    <term id=2 name="red"/>
    <term id=3 name="blue"/>
</term >
```

This is the traditional form of hierarchy familiar from XML 101 examples.

```
<book>
   <chapter>
      <section>
         <paragraph>
            My first XML example.
         </paragraph>
      </section>
   </chapter>
</book>
```

It is likely that if XML is in use within an enterprise, many documents will already include this type of structure. It has the advantage that it is easily understood and directly reflects the two-dimensional nature of traditional Linnean, spreadsheet taxonomies. This makes it very simple to apply XML to an existing vocabulary using ubiquitous tools such as Microsoft Excel. It has the disadvantage of not documenting the relationships of terms other than by their physical placement in the tree. This can be difficult to maintain as the vocabulary grows and becomes more complex. If multiple taxonomy files are combined, this structure is almost certain to be corrupted if not lost altogether.

An alternative to the simple embedded hierarchy is explicitly indicating parent/child relationships with term ids. This simplest approach to this is declaring a "parent" attribute within each node.

```
<term id=1 name="color" />
<term id=2 name="red" parent="1"/>
<term id=3 name="blue" parent="1"/>
```

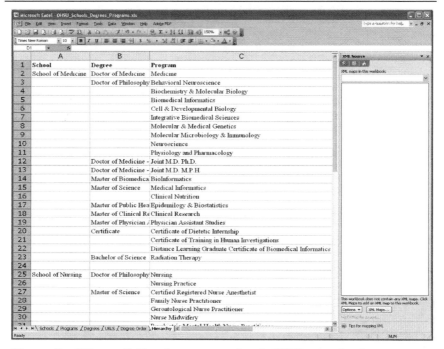

**Figure 3.  Microsoft Excel can map simple XML to a basic taxonomy easily.**

Here, "color" is the top term with "red" and "blue" as sibling child terms. This structure can be extended indefinitely by adding additional nodes or referencing the term id of the appropriate parent term, as in:

<term id=4 name="turquoise" parent="3"/>

This approach has the added advantage of eliminating the need to preserve the order of terms within the taxonomy file. As long as the parent ids are preserved, the taxonomy can be rearranged as desired without disrupting the parent/child relationships. This is particularly useful when combining multiple vocabularies or transforming a taxonomy from one XML format to another, as discussed below.

The parent attribute approach does have a limitation in that it cannot represent polyhierarchies. As declared in the above example, each node can have one and only one parent. Keeping in mind the warnings about entangled hierarchies discussed in the prior chapter, polyhierarchies can be represented by replacing the parent attribute with a new <child> element.

```
<term name="color" id="1">
    <child id="2"/>
    <child id="3"/>
</term>
<term name="red" id="2"/>
<term name="blue" id="3"/>
```

In a sense, this approach represents "two steps forward, one step back." While it makes representing polyhierarchies possible, it also reintroduces embedded hierarchy along with all its maintenance requirements. Sometimes this is unavoidable, but is generally a good indicator that it is time to rework the taxonomy into a faceted vocabulary.

The ability to move beyond simple two-dimensional taxonomies is one of the chief advantages of representing a vocabulary in XML. With careful modeling, any of the basic thesaural relationship can be incorporated into the schema and unambiguously represented in the vocabulary. For example, USE FOR associations between preferred and non-preferred terms may be explicitly captured.

```
<relation>
    <relationType>UF</relationType>  <!- -Use For - ->
        <termId>1020001</termId>
        <termName>Heart Attack</termName>
        <termType>ND</termType>  <!--non-descriptor - ->
</relation>
```

Similarly, linguistic equivalents between vocabularies or even parent languages may be captured as well.

```
<relation>
    <relationType>LE</relationType>
    <termId>4573502</termId>
    <termName>infarto</termName>
    <termType>PT</termType>
    <termLanguage>Spanish</termLanguag>
</relation>
```

As enterprise application become increasingly sophisticated and semantically rich, this flexibility is critical. If a taxonomy is to adequately represent a given domain of knowledge, it must be structured in a manner that accurately reflects that domain. Merely capturing <broaderTerm> <narrowerTerm> relationships is rarely sufficient.

Regardless of the approach taken to represent the structure of the vocabulary, the "id" attribute of each node is critical. Without a unique identifier, it is very difficult to update nodes in the tree and maintain the relationships between nodes when a term changes or becomes obsolete. The identifier can also lead to difficulties when combining vocabularies. In most cases, a term's identifier is only unique within the vocabulary itself. It is entirely possible that terms from different vocabularies will have the same identifier. Any such conflicts must be resolved when more than one vocabulary is used within a single application.

## *Fear of Baggage Handling*

Despite the advantages of capturing the structure of a taxonomy, most organizations are still hesitant to invest the resources necessary to do so. Creating the necessary tags adds a lot of baggage to the vocabulary. After all, even the official XML specification states that "terseness in XML markup is of minimal importance." A single-word term can suddenly explode into a dozen or more lines of XML depending on the complexity of the schema. It is understandable that people are hesitant to try justifying this to management when getting resources to create the taxonomy in the first place is often a hard sell.

```
<DescriptorRecord ...><!-- Descriptor  -->
   <DescriptorUI>D000005</DescriptorUI>
   <DescriptorName><String>Abdomen</String></DescriptorName>
   <Annotation> region & abdominal organs...
   </Annotation>
   <ConceptList>
      <Concept PreferredConceptYN="Y"><!-- Concept  -->
         <ConceptUI>M0000005</ConceptUI>
         <ConceptName><String>Abdomen</String></ConceptName>
         <ScopeNote> That portion of the body that lies
         between the thorax and the pelvis.</ScopeNote>
         <TermList>
            <Term ... PrintFlagYN="Y" ... ><!-- Term  -->
               <TermUI>T000012</TermUI>
               <String>Abdomen</String><!-- String = the term itself -->
               <DateCreated>
                   <Year>1999</Year>
                   <Month>01</Month>
                   <Day>01</Day>
               </DateCreated>
            </Term>
            <Term IsPermutedTermYN="Y" LexicalTag="NON">
                <TermUI>T000012</TermUI>
                <String>Abdomens</String>
            </Term>
         </TermList>
      </Concept>
   </ConceptList>
</DescriptorRecord>
```

**Figure 4. A partial record for the concept "Abdomen" in the MeSH vocabulary.**

Unfortunately, this is another case of "pay me now or pay me later." When every application has its own way of looking at a taxonomy file and every taxonomy has its own way of organizing terms, you have to explain to each and every tool and taxonomy how to talk with each other. This means writing adapters. With the number of available taxonomies growing exponentially, it is keeping many a developer gainfully employed. Adapters are easy to write, and in many cases they are the right approach. However XML can greatly simplify the process.

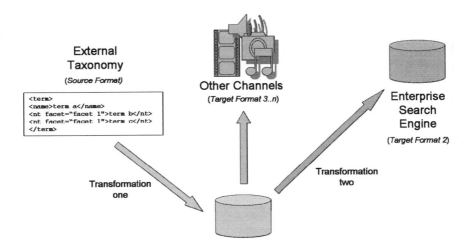

**Figure 5. The secret life of an enterprise taxonomy.**

Without XML, you are required to create a specific adapter for every taxonomy and application that need to interact. If you have four tools that need to share a single taxonomy, you must create and maintain six adapters. This number grows exponentially as the number of taxonomies in use increases. If six partners each want to exchange their own taxonomy with the other members of the group, thirty-six transformations are involved. XML can simplify the process by leveraging XSLT as a commonly understood translation mechanism.

# *XSLT*

The eXtensible Stylesheet Language (XSL) is an XML formatting and transformation language. Its most common application is converting an XML document from one format to another, i.e., converting a spreadsheet to HTML. It does this by breaking up the source document into its basic XML components then comparing each of these pieces to a stylesheet. This stylesheet is basically a collection of templates containing instructions on how to handle a particular part of the source document. The **XSLT processor** could search for column headings and rows in a spreadsheet document and output them as an HTML table or bulleted list.

At a fundamental level, XSLT is about repurposing information. This is especially useful when a taxonomy needs to be applied to an application beyond its original purpose. Nearly all information management tools now claim to "read XML." This means that they can ingest an XML document without too much trouble, but in order to make use of its contents, the document must be in that tool's particular flavor of XML. Either you must map the schema of your vocabulary to the data fields of the application or transform it as a whole into the required format. XSLT enables you to create these transformations in an easily understood and standardized way.

To illustrate, consider applying vocabulary designed for broad application in a rich domain such as medical information and making it usable for a search engine. The Medical Subject Headings (MeSH) is one of the richest vocabularies currently available in any domain. It is intended to be flexible enough to meet the demands of nearly any medical information application. As a result, its schema is very complex, running to several pages. Even the subset of the vocabulary intended for consumer health uses, MedlinePlus, is more sophisticated than is necessary for most search applications. The Medline schema consists of forty elements. The search engine scheme requires only six. As a result, it needs to be pared down to what the search engine can understand.

Here is the XML for a single concept, "Abdominal Pain," in the MedlinePlus XML.

```xml
<MedicalTopic ID="T3061" langcode="English">
    <ID>3061</ID>
    <MedicalTopicName>AbdominalPain</MedicalTopicName>
    <URL>http://www.nlm.nih.gov/medlineplus/abdominalpain.html</URL>
    <DateCreated>01/07/2003</DateCreated>
    <SeeReferencesList>
      <SeeReference>
        <SeeRefName>Pain, Abdominal</SeeRefName>
        <MeshHeadingList>
          <MeshHeading>
             <Descriptor>
                <DescriptorName>Abdominal Pain</DescriptorName>
                <DescriptorUI>D015746</DescriptorUI>
             </Descriptor>
          </MeshHeading>
        </MeshHeadingList>
      </SeeReference>
    </SeeReferencesList>
    <MeshHeadingList>
      <MeshHeading>
         <Descriptor>
            <DescriptorName>Abdominal Pain</DescriptorName>
            <DescriptorUI>D015746</DescriptorUI>
         </Descriptor>
      </MeshHeading>
     </MeshHeadingList>
     <Groups>
       <Group>
          <GroupID>2</GroupID>
          <GroupName>Digestive System</GroupName>
          <GroupURL>http://medlineplus/digestives.html</GroupURL>
       </Group>
     <Group>
          <GroupID>31</GroupID>
          <GroupName>Symptoms</GroupName>
          <GroupURL>http://medlineplus/symptoms.html</GroupURL>
     </Group>

  </Groups>
     <RelatedTopics>
         <RelatedTopic IDREF="T351"/>
     </RelatedTopics>
     <LanguageMappedTopicID>3062</LanguageMappedTopicID>
</MedicalTopic>
```

If the search engine is to be able to ingest and apply this concept, the above XML must be reduced to this.

```
<node name="Abdominal Pain" id="T3061" parent="G31" classify="true">
    <synonym name="T3061" classify="true"/>
</node>
```

XSLT allows you to create a **stylesheet** identifying which elements in the source vocabulary are of interest and providing instruction for where and how to place them in the new vocabulary. In the above example, we only want to preserve four elements: <MedicalTopic>, <ID>, <MedicalTopicName> and <GroupID>. This is just 10% of the available elements. To facilitate this, however, we can take advantage of other elements within the source vocabulary and some of the text manipulation features of XSLT.

The MedlinePlus vocabulary provides all terms in both English and Spanish. The language of a particular term is indicated by the <langcode> element. In the stylesheet you can define a constant with the value "English" to be compared with the <langcode> value of each term in the MedlinePlus vocabulary. If the MedlinePlus term is in English, it will be copied to the new vocabulary. If it is Spanish, it will be ignored. The element label can be transformed in this copying process. In our example <MedicalTopic> becomes <node>, <MedicalTopicName> becomes <name> and <GroupID> becomes <parent>.

The contents of these elements can also be manipulated in the transformation process. In this example, we need to distinctly identify <Groups> within the list of terms. To do this we can simply define a text constant "G" and prepend it to the <GroupID> element as it is copied. Similarly, values that have no corresponding element in the source vocabulary can be added. In this case, we insert the <classify> element with the text value "true" for every term that is added to the new vocabulary.

XSLT 2.0 is a computationally complete programming language. This means that theoretically, any computational task can be accomplished in XSTL (though probably not efficiently, quickly, or easily). This makes it a fairly complex language to learn and apply with any proficiency, especially if your taxonomy application requires any sophisticated transformations or manipulations of the vocabulary. Fortunately, hand-coding XSTL scripts is rarely necessary. Tools have emerged that allow you to visually map the desired transformations and then automatically generate the necessary code (see figure 7). While these tools are not necessarily cheap, the time saved in developing and maintaining XSLT scripts makes them a sound investment.

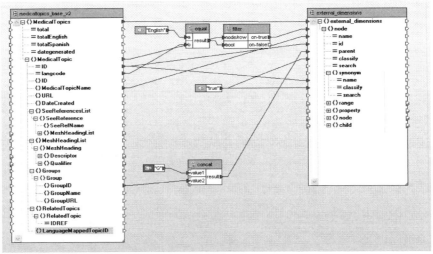

**Figure 6. XMLSpy from Altova.**

Even with the advantages of XML-encoded taxonomies and XSLT transformation, there are still challenges. It's not very difficult to map from XML to XML, but what gets complex is understanding the relationships between different kinds of XML. Some vocabulary authors and publishers may conform to a standard XML-based format, but others will insist on using their own proprietary XML.

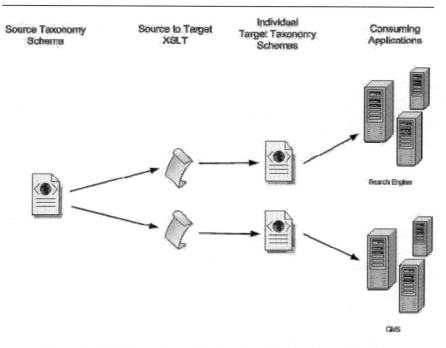

Source Taxonomy Schema     Source to Target XSLT     Individual Target Taxonomy Schemas     Consuming Applications

Search Engine

CMS

**Figure 7. XSLT can dramatically simplify taxonomy sharing.**

This lands us back with the original problem of writing and creating multiple adapters for each taxonomy and application. XSLT simplifies the problem but does not eliminate it.

What is needed is a **staging schema.** This is a common, source-neutral container structure for all taxonomies used in the enterprise. With such a structure in place, applications only need a single transformation from their own schema to that of the staging schema. Likewise, any taxonomy that is to be introduced into the environment only needs to be transformed once. This requires just one XSLT script per source taxonomy regardless of the number of target tools.

At first blush, it may seem desirable to design the staging schema according to the specific needs of the organization free of the constraints imposed by the authors and publishers of the source taxonomies. This seductive option needs to be carefully examined

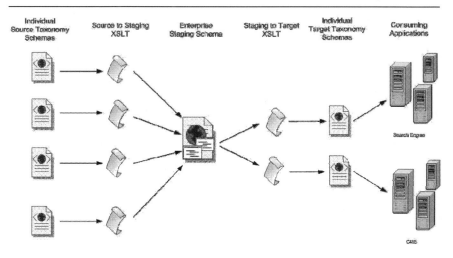

**Figure 8. A staging schema will extend the benefits of XSLT.**

before being adopted. A tailor-made schema will give your applications a custom fit from in-house vocabularies, but will require transformation of anything brought in from the outside. Similarly, any partners outside of the enterprise will need to map or translate your taxonomy schema to their own. While XSLT can simplify this process, adopting a standard can all but eliminate it. That standard has emerged in the form of Zthes.

# *Zthes*

Standard protocols for describing, exchanging and navigating controlled vocabularies have been available for a couple of decades in the form of ANSI/NSO Z39.19 and ISO 2788. Both protocols are pre-Web technologies and their implementation in commercial systems has been inconsistent at best. A single query can return wildly different results even among systems that embrace the protocols. Zthes provides a common implementation of Z39.50 and ISO2788 as an XML schema where all elements are universally defined. This eliminates the need for custom implementations and idiosyncratic interpretations of queries and taxonomies. As a result,

Zthes has opened adoption of the standards to the masses. As vendors, system implementers, and integrators adopt the standard, the need for custom transformations and schemas is rapidly diminishing. If the vocabulary is structured and encoded according to the standard, you can just throw out a taxonomy from one system that speaks Zthes to another and it will just know how to deal with it.

At its core, Zthes is an abstract model for representing vocabularies with a strong emphasis on thesauri. Zthes vocabularies are modeled as a database of inter-linked terms. These links can be between terms in different vocabularies, or even in different physical thesauri. This makes Zthes is particularly well suited to a faceted approach, since any single thesauri can contain multiple individual vocabularies making the overall structure a meta-thesaurus of sorts.

Zthes terms are represented in three parts, a main record and two sub-records. The main record describes the term itself. The first sub-record describes relationships among terms. The second keeps a tally of occurrences of the term within the documents and databases to which the vocabulary is applied. Below is an example Zthes entry created by Factiva for the term "zoology."[2]

The complete Zthes specification may seem like overkill for some applications and woefully inadequate to capture the full semantics of others. The intention of Zthes is to provide a common representation of the most common elements that will satisfy the needs of most applications. It is not necessary to provide a value for every single element in the record. If a source vocabulary has features beyond the ability of Zthes to capture, that's fine. It just means that the additional information will not be available through a Zthes-compliant interface. It can still be used outside the context of Zthes.

Within the main record, only two elements are mandatory, termId and termName. TermId is a unique identifier (again unique only within the current vocabulary) that provides the primary means of navigating the relationships between terms. Even if the source vocabulary does not contain a unique identifier, one must be created for each term that is to be in the Zthes format. TermName, of course, contains the text label of the term itself.

Beyond these two rudimentary elements, Zthes provides a substantial structure for documenting your vocabulary.

**termType**: An indication of the type of the term. It is recommended that the value of this element be restricted to one of three options: Preferred term (PT); Non-descriptor (ND); or Node label (NL). If these prove inadequate, other values can be defined and used. Best practice in this case is to start each of these new extension values with "x-" as in "x-myValue."

**termVocabulary**: This documents the source vocabulary from which the term was drawn. For example, a custom taxonomy of medical conditions could have terms drawn from MeSH, SNOMED, and UMLS. This field will preserve the relationship between the term and its parent vocabulary.

**termCategory**: This field allows you to group terms into topical subsets within the vocabulary. Any term can belong to any number of categories. Similarly, any given category can consist of any number of terms, even if those terms live in different sub-vocabularies of the (meta-) thesaurus.

**termNote**: This is an explanatory note about any aspect of the term that needs documentation. In most cases it is used as a scope note or definition, but since it is a repeatable element with no restrictions on content, it can be applied to any documentation need not covered in the rest of the specification.

In addition to describing the characteristics and behaviors of the terms, Zthes provides a number of administrative elements that facilitate housekeeping.

**termUpdate**: The update status of the record, which may be "add" or "delete."

**termStatus**: The deletion status of the term.

**termApproval**: An indication of whether the term has been approved for inclusion in the thesaurus.

**termCreatedDate**: The date on which the record defining the term was created.

**termCreatedBy**: The name of the person who created the record defining the term.

**termModifiedDate**: The date on which the record defining the term was last modified.

**termModifiedBy**: The name of the person who last modified the record defining the term.

The **relation** sub-record allows you to capture and of the thesaural relationships defined in ISO2788: Narrower Term (NT), Broader Term (BT), Use Instead (USE), Use For (UF), Related Term (RT), and Language Equivalent (LE). In addition to identifying which terms are related and the nature of the association, the strength and importance of the relationship can also be indicated. This is done by providing a numeric value for the weight attribute of the <relation> element as in <relation weight="97">. The value of this attribute will be determined by the weighting scheme of the taxonomy at hand. If multiple Zthes vocabularies are utilized by a particular application, care must be taken to ensure that the various weighting schemes are compatible. If not, they must be reconciled.

The final component of the Zthes model is the postings sub-record. This simply keeps a record of how many times the current terms exist in a particular document or database. This **target** is identified in the sourceDb element. The tally, contained in the <hitCount> element, can optionally be restricted to a particular field within that database or section of the document. As a result, a Zthes term record could have multiple posting sub-records for a single database. For example, there could be one sub-record for the number of times the term "manager" occurs in the employee table of a database and a separate sub-record noting how many times it occurs in the "payroll" table.

In addition to the records for individual terms, a single additional special record may be added to describe the thesaurus as a whole. This record can be extremely useful in the long-term management of the vocabulary, especially if it is to be shared beyond its initial application. The extent of this descriptive record is left up to the vocabularies' authors and managers. Elements that are included, however, must be drawn from the Dublin Core metadata elements as described in Chapter Two. In addition, there is an optional and repeatable <thesNote> element, similar to <termNote>, which can be used as a freeform textual description of any additional documentation not covered by the Dublin Core specification.

Standardization is lowering the barrier to adopting XML for taxonomies, and most published vocabularies are moving in that direction. Taxonomy Warehouse, an online clearinghouse for controlled vocabularies, has adopted Zthes as one of three standard representations for its available taxonomies.

```
<Zthes>
    <term>
        <termId>918964</termId>
        <termName>Zoology</termName>
        <termType>PT</termType>
        <termLanguage>English</termLanguage>
        <termVocabulary>Training Thesaurus</termVocabulary>
        <termStatus>active</termStatus>
        <termApproval>candidate</termApproval>
        <termSortkey>zoology</termSortkey>
        <termNote label="Scope"> A science that deals
                with animals a branch of biology concerned
                with the animal kingdom and its members
                as individuals and classes and with animal
                life and animal morphology together with
                anatomy, physiology, embryology genetics,
                taxonomy, paleontology, ecology, and
                various other sciences in whole or in part.
                </termNote>
        <termNote label="Source">Webster's</termNote>
        <termCreatedDate>2004-
        1209T12:51:46</termCreatedDate>
        <termCreatedBy>dclarke</termCreatedBy>
        <termModifiedDate>20050103T12:35</termModifiedDate>
        <termModifiedBy>dclarke</termModifiedBy>
        <relation weight="150">
            <relationType>NT</relationType>
            <termId>918965</termId>
            <termName>Applied zoology</termName>
            <termType>PT</termType>
            <termLanguage>English</termLanguage>
        </relation>
    </term>
</Zthes>
```

**Figure 9. An example zThes record.**

# 8

# Ontology

Understanding is a path, not a point.
It is a path of connections between
thought and thought; patterns over patterns.
It is relationships.

Richard Saul Wurman

Taxonomies are indispensable to organizing knowledge, but they do have their limits. The associations among concepts captured within a taxonomy bring structure to a knowledge domain, but also tend to unrealistically simplify it. This is an inherent limitation of generic (IsA – X *is a type of* Y) and whole/part relationships. In the real world, much more complex relationships exist and may in fact be critical to certain tasks and applications. Many of these relationships simply cannot be captured within the scope of basic broader/narrower term hierarchies or even the standard thesaural relationships. We may be able to catalog the various facets of some domain exhaustively, but tying them together in semantically interesting ways will still require human intervention and intuition.

This human element is also a major, if subtle, limitation. All knowledge and information captured in a taxonomy is declarative. That is, it must be explicitly stated and recorded as part of the vocabulary if it is to be available to an application. This is true even if we have encoded the taxonomy in a machine-readable representation such as XML and Zthes, as discussed in the prior chapter. Taxonomies are intended to enumerate factual information. They do not capture information that is implied by those enumerated facts or knowledge that may be logically inferred or deduced from them.

Take for example the faceted wine taxonomy described in the prior chapter. Even if we have the characteristics of a "red wine" made in "Oregon" selling for "40–60 dollars" we cannot deduce that it was made in the "Willamette Valley" region of Oregon, that it is a Pinot Noir or that it may go well with veal, because these facts are not specifically and explicitly captured in the taxonomy.

In most situations, this is not an issue. The requirements for most applications can usually be spelled out in sufficient detail that the taxonomy created to support it will capture the necessary information. However, as system requirements and user demands become more and more sophisticated, this will not always be the case. In certain domains, such as the life sciences, in which advances depend on non-intuitive relationships and the integration of complex data sets, advanced relationships and the ability to infer become critical. These are also the foundational principles of the emerging semantic web. To provide these capabilities and to support true semantic applications, it is necessary to move beyond taxonomy to ontology.

## *What Is An Ontology?*

The notion of ontology has its roots in philosophy dating back to the time of Aristotle or before as "the study of existence" or "the nature of being." Over the past few decades the term has been appropriated by computer science to refer to any structured representation of an area of knowledge. This has caused *ontology* to become something of a catch-all term for any attempt to organize information. It is not uncommon to see taxonomy and thesauri referred to as ontology. In the broadest sense, this is accurate, but it doesn't capture the essential qualities of inferenceability, the ability to deduce valid information not explicitly present in the data, and complex relationships.

Essentially, an ontology is a framework that defines a particular set of concepts, the relationships among them, and the nature of those relationships. The most common definition in use today is that an ontology is "an explicit and formal specification of a shared conceptualization."[1] This may sound like metaphysical mumbo-jumbo, but it hits all of the core issues on which semantic applications depend.

First, it is *explicit* in that it defines and details all of the concepts, properties, and constraints that comprise a particular domain. For example, a wine ontology should define the vintner's world. It would catalog all things that are pertinent to wine including type, vintage, source, complements, price, and so forth. It is *formal* because it must be documented in a form that is both machine readable and interpretable. Our wine ontology should be encoded according to some well understood scheme such as XML, RDF, or OWL (to be discussed in detail later). It is a *conceptualization* in that it takes our list of things we are interested in and organizes them into an abstract model that shows how they relate to one another. Finally, it is *shared* because it represents a consensus among the members of the community the ontology is intended to serve.

All of this applies to taxonomy and thesauri, but ontology takes things a step further. Relationships are not just noted as with the broader/narrower or even association relationships of a taxonomy. They are codified into formal classes and subclasses along with the methods for using them. To a greater or lesser extent (depending on the level of formality required), the vocabulary becomes axiomatized. The rules governing the concepts and relationships making up the ontology are codified in a manner that can be translated into logical operations. This means that the terms and definitions defined in the vocabulary can support computation and inference without a human brain pulling the levers.

# *Class Hierarchy, Slots and Facets*

The basic components of an ontology are *classes*, *slots* and *instances*. A class is an abstraction for a set of objects that share common attributes, structure, and behavior. Most of the nodes in a taxonomy will map to classes as long as they represent a concept with an independent existence rather than something that just describes the concept. Wine and cheese are suitable candidates to become classes because they represent common attributes across a large pool of objects and concepts that may be properly considered "wine" or "cheese." Like a taxonomy, classes should be organized into a hierarchy arranging them into a tree of less specific to more specific concepts. Each child node in the tree is a subclass of its parent and inherits all of its attributes.

Say we have a small taxonomy of cheeses:

```
Cheese
        Soft
                Brie
                Muenster
                Roquefort
        Semi-soft
                Asadero
                Colby
                Quesa Fresca
        Semi-hard
                Cheddar
                Gouda
                Jarlsberg
        Hard
                Asiago
                Gruyere
                Romano
```

Each of the nodes in this tree is a class or subclass. Every concept in the list inherits the properties associated with the cheese class, but each also has properties that distinguish it from its siblings. A soft cheese is distinct from a semi-hard cheese and a gruyere has attributes and behaviors that set it apart from a muenster, but they are all cheeses. Similarly, there are many different Asiago cheeses such as Veneto, Friuli-Venezia and Giulia. The difference between these and the class of cheeses or subclass of asiago cheeses is that you can actually eat these. Friuli-Venezia is an **instance** of the asiago subclass. It is the thing that actually exists, is described by the class and that you can pop in your mouth. Wine is a class. Red Wine is a subclass. "*Giacosa Barolo La Rocche Falletto Riserva 2001*" is an instance. Instances are the terminal nodes in a taxonomy.

The class hierarchy goes a long way to structuring a knowledge domain, but in order to be useful, the internal structure of the classes themselves must be described. Each class has distinct properties that distinguish it from other concepts. In ontology-speak, these properties are called **slots.** If you have conducted a facet analysis of your domain, as described in Chapter Six, you will already have identified many of the slots for your ontology. Generally, slots will fall into one of four categories: intrinsic, extrinsic, parts, and relationships.[2]

Intrinsic properties are those that are inherent in the class itself, like the flavor of a cheese or the milk type from which it is made. Extrinsic slots are those that are not fundamental to the nature of the class but are still an important characteristic, such as name or area of origin. Parts are particularly important if the structure of the object is relevant. These can be physical components such as "rind" or "core" but may also be more abstract, such as the "course" in a meal. Finally, relationship slots are what truly set an ontology apart from other controlled vocabularies. These slots are what allow any association to be modeled regardless of where the participating classes are defined in the ontology. For example, a dairy or creamery is likely to exist in a separate taxonomy or class hierarchy from a pear, apple, or more generally the idea of fruit. However, there may be interesting associations to be had between these disparate concepts. Perhaps a dairy farm and a pear orchard wish to do a joint promotion. A portion of the ontology supporting this could look something like the following (boxes representing instances are shaded):

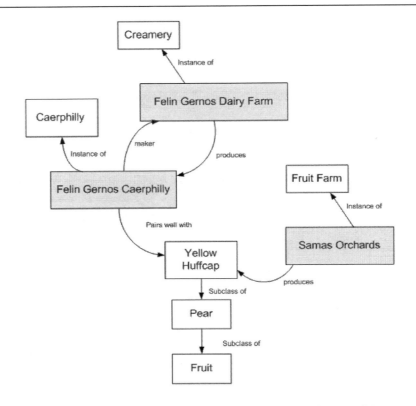

**Figure 1. Ontologies can make inferred relationships possible.**

Notice that there is a path from the "Felin Gernos Dairy Farm" to the "Samas Orchards" via the relationship "pairs well with." Because the relationships are explicitly captured, an inference engine (software that can "reason" and make decisions based on logical inference) would be able to discover this potential collaborative relationship, even if the people at each organization were unaware of it. Also notice that relationship types are reused. The "produces" association is applicable to both dairy products and fruits.

A final requirement of slots is that their domain and range be defined. The **range** of a slot is simply the classes that may be used to populate it. For example, "cheese" may be the only allowable class for the "produces" slot. If so, then the range of the slot is the class "cheese." **Domain** goes the other direction, covering the classes a particular slot describes. In our example above, both the "Creamery" and "Fruit Farm" classes are attached, via their instances, to the "produces" slot so its domain is those two classes.

The last aspect of slots that must be addressed is the assignment of their facets. These are the actual values that are available for the slots. If you have created a faceted classification scheme, most of the work is done. Each facet becomes a slot and the terms of the facet become the values of the slot. For example, we may have identified three slots for our base class "cheese": "Moisture Level," "Flavor," and "Milk." These three properties are possessed by every type of cheese so they belong in the base-class where they will be inherited by every subclass or type of cheese. The acceptable values of these properties become the facet of the slot.

### Cheese Slots

Moisture level
    Low
    Medium
    High
Flavor
    Mild
    Strong
    Sharp
Milk
    Cow
    Goat
    Sheep

Once the ontology is modeled and populated with instances you have created a **knowledgebase**. There are currently tens of thousands of knowledgebases and data sets structured in this manner, many of them openly available on the web. Even with this large number, any ontology or knowledge base can be classified as one of four basic types. Li Ding of the University of Baltimore has detailed out these four categories as follows. [3]

## Meta-Ontologies

The ontology languages, namely RDF, RDFS, DAML+OIL and OWL, are in fact meta-ontologies themselves; and their instances are Semantic Web ontologies. Such meta-ontologies offer a small vocabulary and corresponding axioms as the building blocks for any conceptualisms, and they are backed by inference engines with built-in support for their ontology constructs and axioms.

## Comprehensive Upper Ontologies

Upper ontologies provide a high-level model about the world using the ontology constructs provided by the meta-ontologies.

## Systematic Domain Specific Ontologies

Unlike upper ontologies which require agreements across multiple domains, *domain specific ontologies* have been developed to build systematic vocabulary for certain domains long before the inception of the Semantic Web, e.g., legal ontology, gene ontology, chemical ontology, bio ontology, and spatial ontology. Domain ontologies can also contain some well known class instances besides class/property definition, e.g., an airport ontology not only defines the class "airport," but also enumerates all three-letter airport codes.

## Simple Specialized Ontologies

One difficulty with comprehensive or systematic ontologies is that they are usually too big to use. For example, no existing ontology inference engine can store and use the complete OpenCyc ontology, which has over 60,000 terms and is stored in a 700MB file. Hence, many simple specialized semantic Web ontologies have been developed to overcome this difficulty by concentrating on a set of basic and commonly-used concepts. Such ontologies are often used as interchange languages in knowledge sharing.

These four categories are the essence of the semantic web. Most of the work that will go into creating semantic applications will occur at the level of simple specialized ontologies. Anyone who creates or uses a semantic application will be taking advantage of meta-ontologies and to a certain extent upper ontologies, but most of this will be completely transparent.

The process of building an ontology extends the information organization principles fundamental to taxonomy. As we've noted throughout this book, bits and pieces of data are rarely useful in and of themselves. In order to make sense of things, we need to place the data we encounter in some context. Meaning comes from the relationships between things. This applies to both concrete objects and abstract notions. Humans do this by creating mental models. In our minds, each of us has a set of templates that have been built up over the course of our lifetimes. Our daily experiences, even those involving new, unknown and novel experiences, are compared to our mental models and interpreted according to the world view they support. The reasoning ability this process facilitates is perhaps the prime factor keeping human intelligence ahead of machine intelligence. Ontologies and the semantic web are aimed at closing this gap. Humans build, modify and extend our mental models unconsciously. In order for a machine or a piece of software to make use of data and information, it must be provided with an explicit model of how each piece of information relates to all other bits of data it will encounter. This is the basic notion behind an ontology and more broadly a data model of any sort.

In a data model, a well defined set of information is organized for a well defined set of functions in a well defined application. This is the underpinning principal of the databases that currently drive the World Wide Web and most business applications. Unfortunately, this traditional approach to organizing data is not up to the demands of advanced semantic applications. A more flexible data model is necessary to capture the structure of an ontology in a consistent and comprehensive way. Enabling this description through a simple meta-model and advanced metadata is the function of the **Resource Description Framework (RDF)**.

# *Resource Description Framework*

The basic concept of an RDF data model is simple. Everything is described in terms of **resources** and **statements.** A resource is basically anything that can be identified and referenced. This may be a document or file, but it can also be something more abstract that cannot necessarily be retrieved but can still be referred to or discussed. In order for resources to be useful there must be a standard and well understood method of identifying both the resource itself and its current location. The general solution for this is Uniform Resource Identifiers (URI), the most common implementation of which is the Uniform Resource Locator (URL). URLs are structured in such a way that a number of protocols, such as HTTP, SOAP and FTP, can be accommodated allowing a limited set of instructions and commands to be issued between various components of the Web without concern for how they will be interpreted on the receiving end. A statement is similar to a row in a relational database table, except that in RDF the row always has three components (with one exception we will discuss later): a **subject**, a **predicate** and an **object**. Because of this three-part structure, an RDF statement is often referred to as a **triple**.

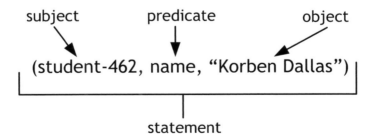

Visually this can be represented by a directed graph.

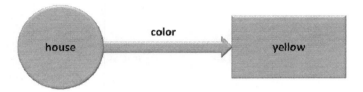

This graph roughly translates to "a yellow house." In RDF we need to refer to a specific house rather than just "house" so the above graph would actually look like the following, which would be something like "the resource identified as house-89 is yellow."

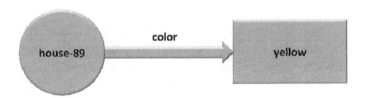

The easiest way to understand an RDF statement is to think back to English class in grade school. The thing being referred to by the statement is the subject. The property of that thing being described is the predicate. The value of that property is the object. In the figure above, something identified as "student-462" has a properly called name that has the value of "Korben Dallas." This maps nicely to the relational tables mentioned above. For example, the row of the Person table representing Mr. Dallas could be translated directly into RDF triples.

| Key | Name | Address | City | State | Phone | Age | Occupation |
|-----|------|---------|------|-------|-------|-----|------------|
| 1 | Korben Dallas | 642 42$^{nd}$ St. | 1 | 1 | (212) 62... | 37 | Cab Driver |

> (Person-1, name, "Korben Dallas")
> (Person-1, address, "642 42$^{nd}$ Street")
> (Person-1, city, "Pittsburgh")
> (Person-1, state, "Pennsylvania")
> (Person-1, age, "37")
> (Person-1, occupation, "Cab Driver")

This is pretty straightforward, but you may have noticed a few discrepancies. First, we have no dedicated triple representing the column "Key." In our RDF statements, the primary key of the Person table that corresponds with "Korben Dallas" is "1" uniquely identifying Mr. Dallas *in that table*. Any other table in the database that wishes to refer to Mr. Dallas will do so with this value referencing that table (a foreign key). RDF uniquely identifies Mr. Dallas with a URI reference. This could take the form of something like:

> http://www.fifthelementcabs.com/1997/personnel/0647_Dallas

This will uniquely identify a resource representing Mr. Dallas regardless of what is referring to him and from where. URIs can get pretty cumbersome to work with when completely spelled out (not to mention unreadable) so they are often replaced with short names or labels such as "name" or "person" when modeling. It is important to remember that an actual RDF application will store and process the full URI. To illustrate, consider an RDF triple from the above example.

> (Person-1, city, "Pittsburgh")

"Person-1" and "city" are shorthand labels that make it simple for a human to read and understand the statement. The actual statement would look more like:

(http://aim.uoregon.edu/SemanticWeb/definitions/summer2010/Unit2/Person,http://www.w3c.org/proposals/06/1809/2005/rdf/definitions/city,"Pittsburgh)

There are a couple of additional ways to identify a unique resource in an RDF model or on the semantic web. You can simply say that one resource is the same as another. Not equivalent to, but the same. More importantly, it is possible to infer identity based on other statements. For example, Oregon Health & Science University had only one president during the period of 1995–2006. If it is known that a certain person was president of OHSU during that time, then he would be uniquely identified, by virtue of that relationship, even if his name is never explicitly mentioned or referenced. Multiple properties and relationships can also be represented graphically.

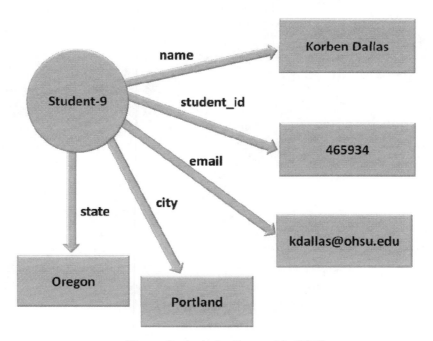

**Figure 2. A student record in RDF.**

Think of the graph in figure 2 as representing a single row in a STUDENT database table. The table will have columns for name, student_id, email, city and state. The corresponding RDF is represented in the graph. Resources are represented as ovals. The rectangles represent **literals**, or basically strings of characters assigned to each property.

In many situations it is not necessary to identify a resource. You may wish to refer to "a cab driver in Pittsburgh," "that student," or "a graduate course." Such **anonymous resources** are possible in RDF and come in quite handy as we will see. Such unidentified resources are called **blank nodes** or **b-nodes**.

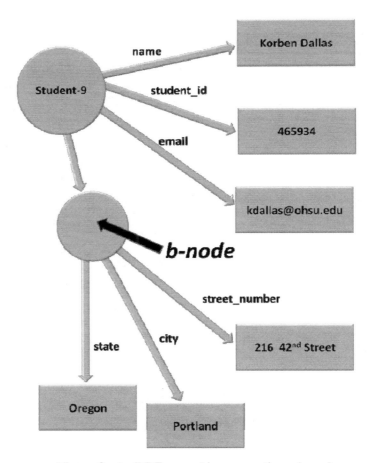

**Figure 3. An RDF record incorporating a b-node.**

For example, in figure 2 above there are city and state resources but they have no relationship to each other beyond the fact that this particular student has one of each. In reality we know that a city is located within a state and that together they comprise a location or part of an address. It probably isn't useful to uniquely identify this notion of address, but relating its components might make them easier to manage. We can accomplish this with a b-node (see figure 3).

If we discover that this particular grouping is going to be frequently useful in various and sundry situations we can declare it as a particular type specifying that an ADDRESS always has a STREET-NUMBER, CITY and STATE.

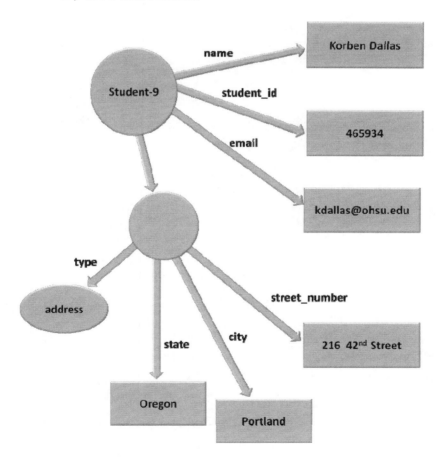

**Figure 4.  A persistently identified email account.**

In some cases, groupings of this sort should be uniquely identified. For example, a system administrator may be concerned with email accounts as a way of grouping information, but she also has a need to keep track of specific accounts, each with its own set of information (such as the associated email address, the date the account was created and so forth). In this case, the grouping node receives a unique identifier such as email-account-607 in the graph below.

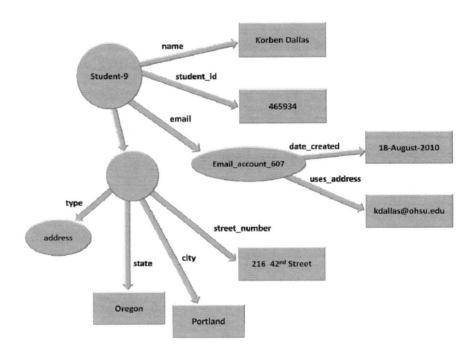

**Figure 5. An RDF graph grouping components for reuse.**

One of the quirkier aspects of RDF is its approach to making statements about statements themselves. If you wish to comment on a certain assertion, say, "The statement that Korben Dallas is a cab driver is false," RDF does not provide a way to directly reference the original statement. In other words, a statement cannot be the subject of another statement. RDF does, however, let you get there in a bit of a roundabout way. Normally, an RDF triple is not considered a resource. However, it is possible to declare a resource of type "Statement" and give it a URI.

Look at the graph below. It basically says, "There is something with type RFD:Statement that has 'person-1' as its subject, 'name' as its predicate and 'Korben Dallas' as its object." (In practice, each of these would actually be a fully qualified URI). This newly created "thing" can now be the subject of other statements. This process of making a resource out of a statement is called **reification**, basically making something abstract concrete—making it real. This technique is one of the cornerstones of semantic applications.

If you attempt to create an RDF model of anything beyond the simple examples you have seen here, it will quickly become apparent that things get very complex, very quickly. It is not uncommon for a "small" triple-store to contain over a million records. You will also notice that there is a lot of repetition and redundancy in your model. A nice, clean, normalized relational database will generally seem much simpler to create, understand and maintain. So the question arises, why bother with RDF?

The short answer is flexibility. There are many things you can do in RDF that simply can't be done, at least not easily, in a conventional database. A few examples given by consultant and RDF advocate Thomas Passin include[4]:

- Combine the data with other data sets that don't follow the data model you have been using.

- Add more data that doesn't fit the table structures. You could add a book's

- Exchange data with any other application that knows how to handle RDF. You can do this over the Web, by email, or any other way by which you can exchange a data file. There is no equivalent way to exchange the data in a relational database.

- Use an RDF processor that can do logical reasoning to discover unstated relationships in the data.

- Use someone else's ontology to learn more about the relationships between the properties and resources in your data.

- Add statements about publications and references that have been defined somewhere else on the Web. All you have to do is to refer to the identifiers (the URIs) that they have published. You aren't limited to talking about things stored in your own database.

- Do all these things using well defined standards, so that a wide range of software can process the data.

This list is by no means comprehensive, but it should give you an idea of the motivations behind representing knowledge, information and data in the RDF. Despite this power, it is critical to remember that RDF is at its heart a data model. Once we have structured our information this way, we still need a way to represent data that can be consumed by machines and their applications. As you may have guessed from the prior chapter, XML is the key to this representation, specifically RDF-Schema (RDFS).

# *RDF/XML*

Once your information is organized into a model that a human can understand, it must be encoded in a manner that software can interpret. This means that its representation must adhere to a well defined syntax. RDF/XML provides this syntax for representing RDF triples. As an example, the statement, "The Web page at

http://aim.uoregon.edu/semweb/index.html

has a publish-date of August 19, 2010," could be represented as the following triple:

(index.html, publish-date "August 19, 2010")

which in turn could be represented in RDF as:

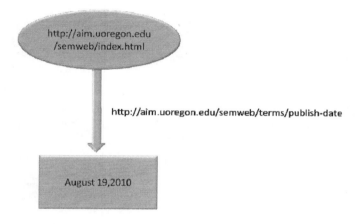

In order for this statement to be of use on the semantic web, it must be represented in a machine-readable form. A possible representation in XML would be:

```
<?xml version="1.0"?>
 <rdf:RDF
        xmlns:rdf="http://www.w3.org/1999/02/22-
        rdf-syntax-ns#"
        xmlns:aimterms="http://aim.uoregon.edu/
        semweb/terms/">

        <rdf:Description
             rdf:about="http://aim.uoregon.edu
          /semweb/index.html">
  <aimterms:publish-date>August 19, 2010
        </aimterms:publish-date>
  </rdf:Description>
  </rdf:RDF>
```

This is essentially the bare minimum representation for a machine-interpretable statement. As you can see there is a lot of apparent overhead involved with semantic markup. This is somewhat unavoidable, but each piece of the code does serve a purpose.

```
<?xml version="1.0"?>
```

This is the XML declaration indicating that the document is in XML and what version of XML is being used.

```
<rdf:RDF
 xmlns:rdf="http://www.w3.org/1999/02/22-rdf-syntax-ns#
 xmlns:aimterms="http://aim.uoregon.edu/semweb/terms/">
```

This is the beginning of the RDF element. Everything between this point and the closing </rdf:RDF> tag represents RDF. The xmlns attribute begins a namespace declaration as described in the prior chapter. In this case, the namespace points at the RDF namespace, so everything in this document that is prefixed with rdf: is defined in the RDF vocabulary identified by http://www.w3.org/1999/02/22-rdf-syntax-ns#. This is the standard RDF schema maintained by W3C. The xmlns:aimterms attribute points to another RDF vocabulary, most likely a locally defined schema. Everything in the current document prefixed with aimterms refers to elements defined in the aimterms vocabulary.

```
<rdf:Description
   rdf:about="http://aim.uoregon.edu/semweb/index.html">
      <aimterms:publish-date>August 19, 2010
      </aimterms:publish-date>
</rdf:Description>
```

This is the meat of the actual RDF statement in RDF/XML. At its core, every RDF statement is a description of something. The description is about the subject of the statement. Here the statement is about http://aim.uoregon.edu/semweb/index.html and gives it a property of publish-date with the value of "August 19, 2010." RDF/XML uses this simple description/about model for all of its basic statements, adding additional properties to flesh out the description of any given subject.

```
</rdf:RDF>
```

This closing tag indicates the conclusion of the RDF statement. This is a lot of overhead text, but it doesn't all have to be repeated for every attribute you may wish to add to a statement. The following example adds an additional namespace, "dc" for the Dublin Core, and uses that namespace to assign an additional property, language, to the same resource described in the previous example.

```
<?xml version="1.0"?>
  <rdf:RDF xmlns:rdf="http://www.w3.org/1999/02/22-rdf-syntax-ns#"
    xmlns:dc="http://purl.org/dc/elements/1.1/"
    xmlns:aimterms="http://aim.uoregon.edu/semweb/terms/">

  <rdf:Description
    rdf:about="http://aim.uoregon.edu/semweb/index.html">
      <aimterms:publish-date>
          August 19, 2010
      </aimterms:publish-date>
  </rdf:Description>

<rdf:Description
    rdf:about="http://aim.uoregon.edu/semweb/index.html">
          <dc:language>en</dc:language>
</rdf:Description>

        </rdf:RDF>
```

# *RDF Schema*

One of the foundations of semantics is shared vocabulary. Without a common understanding of terminology, it is impossible to arrive at a shared understanding of meaning. RDF provides a way to model information, and RDF/XML provides a syntax for describing that model in a machine-interpretable manner, but neither provide a way to define vocabularies for particular knowledge domains. For example, we can declare a property creation date in RDF and represent it in RDF/XML, but we have no way of defining the range of values that can be used within that property. A user could use "August, 19, 2010," "8/19/2010," "xyz," or "Genesis 1:6" with equal validity. The possible values within a given domain and the relationships among them must be clearly defined and understood by all users of a system, both human and machine. Without that capability, the semantic Web is meaningless (no pun intended). Defining these structured vocabularies is the role of **RDF Schema (RDFS)**.

RDFS defines vocabularies in terms of classes and properties. For example, we may wish to describe a class aimterms:course and assign it properties such as aimterms:instructor, aimterms:enrollment, aimterms:semester and so forth. Now rather than discussing a specific *instance* of a course we can discuss a whole group of things that share common characteristics. Just as importantly, we can create specialized types of these things as subclasses of this group. These subclasses share the basic characteristics of the parent class, but can also have properties that distinguish it. For example, we may create aimterms:short_course, aimterms:online_course, and aimterms:onsite_course as subclasses of aimterms:course. This means that each of these subclasses will inherit the properties aimterms:instructor, aimterms:enrollment, aimterms:semester, but will have additional properties that distinguish them: aimterms:online_course may have aimterms:course_url for example.

These hierarchies of classes and properties are the core of the semantic Web. By understanding the terms and relationships inherent in a particular knowledge domain, it becomes possible to reason over that domain in novel ways. RDFS is the first step toward this shared understanding. It provides a rudimentary way to express ontology.

# *Web Ontology Language (OWL)*

As we have said throughout this chapter, the goal of ontologies, and in fact the semantic Web as a whole, is to represent information in a way that gives it explicit meaning so that it can be easily processed and integrated by machines and software agents. RDF and RDFS are a start but do not go far enough. The W3C explains the roles of the languages we have discussed so far quite succinctly.[5]

- XML provides a surface syntax for structured documents, but imposes no semantic constraints on the meaning of these documents.

- XMLS is a language for restricting the structure of XML documents and also extends XML with datatypes.

- RDF is a datamodel for objects ("resources") and relations between them and provides a simple semantics for this datamodel. These datamodels can be represented in an XML syntax.

- RDFS is a vocabulary for describing properties and classes of RDFS resources, with a semantics for generalization hierarchies of such properties and classes.

Any language intended to facilitate the goals of the semantic Web must provide: 1) a well defined syntax, 2) formal semantics, 3) convenience of expression, 4) efficient reasoning support and 5) sufficient expressive power.[6] It is these final two requirements that are not sufficiently supported by RDF and RDFS. The **Web Ontology Language (OWL)** has been designed to fill the gap. Again, according to the W3C:

- OWL adds more vocabulary for describing properties and classes: among others, relations between classes (e.g., disjointness), cardinality (e.g., "exactly one"), equality, richer typing of properties, characteristics of properties (e.g., symmetry), and enumerated classes.

OWL has three increasingly expressive sublanguages designed for use by specific communities of implementers and users.[7]

   • **OWL Lite** supports those users primarily needing a classification hierarchy and simple constraints. For example, while it supports cardinality constraints, it only permits cardinality values of 0 or 1. It should be simpler to provide tool support for OWL Lite than its more expressive relatives, and OWL Lite provides a quick migration path for thesauri and other taxonomies. Owl Lite also has a lower formal complexity than OWL DL.

   • **OWL DL** supports those users who want the maximum expressiveness while retaining computational completeness (all conclusions are guaranteed to be computable) and decidability (all computations will finish in finite time). OWL DL includes all OWL language constructs, but they can be used only under certain restrictions (for example, while a class may be a subclass of many classes, a class cannot be an instance of another class).

   • **OWL Full** is meant for users who want maximum expressiveness and the syntactic freedom of RDF with no computational guarantees. For example, in OWL Full a class can be treated simultaneously as a collection of individuals and as an individual in its own right. OWL Full allows an ontology to augment the meaning of the pre-defined (RDF or OWL) vocabulary. It is unlikely that any reasoning software will be able to support complete reasoning for every feature of OWL

While OWL is not a direct extension of RDFS, it does build on the basic principles of RDF and RDFS. In most cases it is expressed in RDF/XML, but may also be represented with a more human-friendly XML syntax. The W3C's OWL specification uses a more compact, abstract representation that is also a bit easier to follow than the strict RDF/XML approach. Finally, OWL can be represented graphically in much the way RDF graphs are generally presented. The preferred approach is based on the Unified Modeling Language (UML) that has become something of a universal standard for complex modeling.

The graphic approach is the most useful to modelers and knowledge architects because you should never need to directly code OWL (or RDF for that matter). Powerful and intuitive tools are emerging that allow you to build your knowledge model graphically and then generate OWL code (see figure 12). However, the best of these tend to be quite expensive. Free tools are also available that get the job done but tend to be somewhat unstable. The most commonly used of these open source tools is Protégé, developed and maintained by Stanford University. There is a large Protégé use community that is very open to assisting newbies. There is also substantial training available.

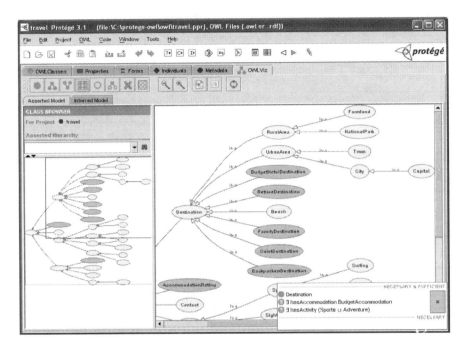

**Figure 6. Protege OWLViz, which can be used to visualize OWL ontologies graphically.**

# 9

# Folksonomy

Do not go where the path may lead, go instead
where there is no path and leave a trail.

-Ralph Waldo Emerson

Landscape architects and park planners go to great pains to ensure
visitors to their spaces can get from point A to point B with ease.
Carefully paved paths are laid out between the duck pond, the
information kiosk and the hot dog stand to make sure people don't
get lost, traipse through the mud or walk on the grass. Yet, despite
our best efforts to anticipate pedestrian's needs, people will always
want to go somewhere else and will have their own way of getting
there. Soon a new route emerges as a trail of bare, packed dirt.
These informal pathways, or **desire lines,** usually emerge in close
proximity to "official" routes. Often they will actually cross paved
sidewalks and clearly marked roads. This does not necessarily mean
that the planners and architects got it wrong. You just can't always
force people to walk where you want them to walk.

Desire lines emerge in information spaces just as they do in physical
spaces. Even the cleverest information architecture and the most
insightful taxonomies will not mesh seamlessly and comprehensively

with the mental models of each and every user. Manifestations of this fact range from sticky-note cheat sheets on computer monitors to private bookmarks for the important parts of an intranet. Whether it is finding a shortcut through the park or a shortcut through a filing system, people make sense of their environment and how they navigate through it in their own way.

**Figure 1. Desire Lines** (photo Phil Gyford)

An interesting aspect of desire lines in public places is that they reflect an unspoken consensus. If one person walks across a lawn, their trail will disappear. The only way for that shortcut to grow into a permanent, if informal, path is for it to be consistently trodden for a reasonable length of time by a significant number of people. This same dynamic is at work in our information spaces as well in the form of **tagging, ethnoclassification** and **folksonomy**.

# *Tagging*

The problem of InfoGlut discussed in Chapter One is not restricted to public and corporate information. Keeping track of personal media and information can be just as challenging. Consider the digital photos no doubt residing on your hard drive. In the old days, organizing family memories consisted of sending out rolls of film to be developed into hardcopy, throwing out pictures of the lens cap and your thumb (roughly eighty percent of each roll) and gluing the surviving pictures into bound volumes. Today, the process usually amounts to plugging in a USB cable and pushing the 'transfer' button.

The problem arises when you want to find that one particular image of Aunt Cindy at your kid's fourth birthday party. Most cameras and computers let you set a default filename for the pictures you transfer, such as kids-bday2007, and then automatically append a unique number for each image. The party pictures will end up in your collection labeled as kids-bday2007_1, kids-bday2007_2, kids-bday2007_3, and so on. Inevitably, you will forget to change the default label each time you transfer photos until you notice that the latest picture is labeled kids_bday2007_8462. In order to find that special picture of your Auntie, you now need to search through 8462 images of everything from the birthday party to the damaged headlight from your wife's fender-bender. If only you had taken the time to add a few descriptive keywords to each image when you copied them. This problem encapsulates the core value proposition of the website flickr.com.

Flickr was created February of 2004 as an online repository for storing and sharing personal images. The key selling point of the service is the ability to organize photos in your own way. According to the flickr.com information page:

> In Flickr, you can give your friends, family, and other contacts permission to organize your photos - not just to add comments, but also notes and tags. People like to ooh and ahh, laugh and cry, make wisecracks when sharing photos. Why not give them the ability to do this when they look at them over the internet? And as all this info accretes around the photos as metadata, you can find them so much easier later on, since all this info is also searchable.

Tagging has proven to be the secret sauce that makes flickr tick. A **tag**, in this context, is simply a keyword added to a photo by the user. The difference between these tags and the formal metadata we have discussed to this point is its audience. Whereas formal metadata needs to hold meaning for an entire community, tags need only be meaningful to the individual creating them. People add tags to content for a wide variety of purposes.[1]

- **Identifying what (or who) it is about.**  First and foremost, people use tags to identify subjects. Common and proper nouns describe the topic or subject of a resource to a greater or lesser degree of specificity.

- **Identifying what it is.**  These tags group resources by kind, such as review, blog, wiki, etc.

- **Identifying who owns it.**  Sometimes identifying who created or maintains a resource is just as important as what that resource contains. The author of a blog or the holder of a copyright is often critical information.

- **Refining categories.**  People will often add tags to content that refine or qualify other groupings, rather than establishing a new category.

- **Identifying qualities or characteristics.**  Similar to refining categories, these tags express the user's personal reaction or opinion to the content. Adjectives such as funny, scary, confusing, and even conspiracy, false and truth are common tags.

- **Self reference.**  People like to use tags to keep track of their stuff. Tags like me, mylinks, suzans_pictures, and the like serve as a virtual filing system for personal resources wherever they may be located.

- **Task organizing.**  In addition to keeping track of useful resources, people also like to remind themselves of what they intended to do with them. Tags that indicate a task to perform or that has been completed, for example to_read,  delete, and send_to_office, extend the virtual filing to become a virtual day-planner.

Consider flickr images A, B, and C along with their associated tags.

## Flickr Image A

| | |
|---|---|
| mlk | public_domain |
| martin_luther_king | pingnews |
| african-american | shapinsky |
| making history | pingnews.com |
| racism | royalty-free |
| portrait | stock |
| candid | photo |
| american_history | stockfoto |
| American | digital |
| Marion_S_Trikosko | archive |
| Trikosko | shapinsky |

## Flickr Image B

| | |
|---|---|
| tag1 | delete |
| tag2 | save |
| taggedout | save2 |
| piano | delete2 |
| keys | savedbydmu |
| white | canon |
| black | powershot |
| macro | a610 |
| close-up | photoshop |

## Flickr Image C

| | |
|---|---|
| me | spring break |
| happy | Georgia |
| elated | school |
| of me | USA |
| 365days | 095/366 |
| self-portrait | 366of2008 |
| teacher | |

Image A is a candid photograph of Dr. Martin Luther King Jr. Several of the tags capture the subject of the photo with varying degrees of specificity. mlk and martin_luther_king pinpoint the individual while African-american and American-history represent much broader categories but could still be considered the subject of the picture. Other tags related to the picture itself rather than its content. public_domain, royalty-free, stockfoto and archive all have something to do with the photo as an object and how it may be used. The tags Marion_S_Trikosko and shapinsky will probably not be meaningful to the casual browser unless they happen to know that Marin Trikosko was a photographer at the heart of the American civil rights movement or that D. F. Shapinsky runs a content aggregation service called pingnews.com. Those tags will, however, be useful to the person who added them to the image of Dr. King.

Several of the tags associated with Image B are similar in nature to those just discussed. Piano and keys are descriptive of the subject, while canon, powershot, a610 and photoshop are all indicative of how the image was created. The other tags, save, delete or savedbydmu seem intended to facilitate information management by individual users. Some of the hazards of such **free-tagging** are apparent in labels such as tag1 and tag2. These may have some specific, arcane meaning to the individual who added them, but more likely they are metadata flotsam; tags added as placeholders and promptly forgotten.

Image C represents the most common usage of tags in the flickr universe, keeping track of personal photos. As of December 2010, flickr contained 68,785,594 images carrying the tag me. This is a perfect example of the virtual, personal filing system application of tags. It not only captures the subject (at least for the person creating the tag) of the image, but also its kind, self-portrait, when it was taken, spring break, 366of2008, where, school, Georgia, USA and even the state of mind of the subject, happy, elated.

In all three of these examples, the person adding any given tag was probably doing so for their own purposes. However, when all of those personal tags merge with the greater pool of tags contributed by all users, something interesting emerges from the aggregate, namely a **folksonomy**.

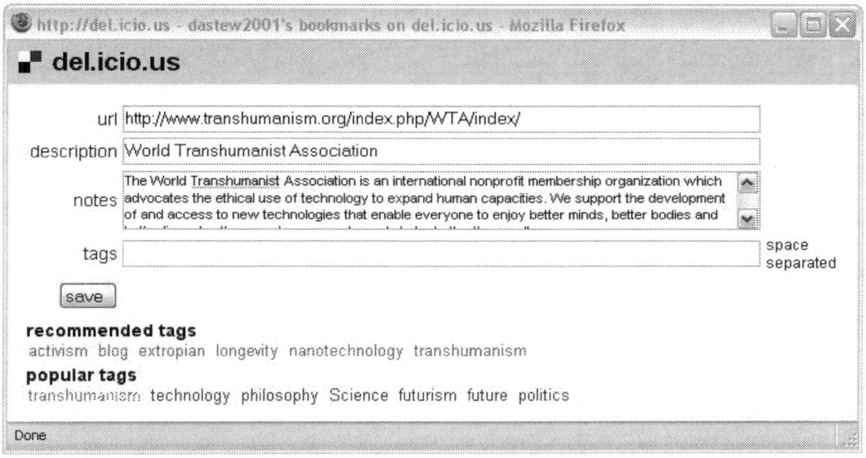

**Figure 2. The tagging interface for del.icio.us.**

## *Folksonomy*

When one person tags something, they are organizing their "stuff." When a large group of people tag that same object, they are engaging in what sociologist Susan Leigh Star has dubbed **ethnoclassification**.[2] As certain tags become increasingly popular for a certain resource, the body of people tagging it are, in essence, collectively deciding what that resource is and where it belongs in the collective understanding of the community. As the number of resources and concepts classified by this implied consensus grows, patterns and informal relationships among terms emerge. The vocabulary these patterns represent has come to be called a folksonomy.

The term folksonomy was first coined by Thomas Vander Wal in an online discussion of ad-hoc labeling and tagging systems. In response to a question as to whether there was a name for informal social classification, Vander Wal responded with a question of his own.

> So the user-created bottom-up categorical structure development with an emergent thesaurus would become a folksonomy?[3]

The term itself is still controversial, but the meme it represents has become integral to the online information landscape. This is understandable as tags and folksonomies attempt to address some of the same fundamental issues as taxonomies and formal metadata in a much easier and cheaper way. This has caused some web design pundits to become passionate advocates of social tagging and folksonomy. The comments of David Sifry are typical of this school of thought.

> Tags are a simple, yet powerful, social software innovation. Today millions of people are freely and openly assigning metadata to content and conversations. Unlike rigid taxonomy schemes that people dislike, the ease of tagging for personal organization with social incentives leads to a rich and discoverable folksonomy. Intelligence is provided by real people from the bottom-up to aid social discovery. And with the right tag search and navigation, folksonomy outperforms more structured approches to classification.[4]

As we will see, establishing "the right tag search and navigation" is easier said than done, but there is something compellingly democratic about emergent vocabularies. In one sense, folksonomy systems follow the term gathering methods of formal taxonomies but cut out the middle man. Rather than trawling search logs and email subject lines for keywords, they are supplied directly and explicitly by content authors and consumers. This may be bottom-up vocabulary creation in the truest sense of the word.

There is also an appeal in the flat nature of a folksonomy. Establishing strict parent-child relationships is difficult and most people have neither the ability nor inclination to build those structures. When a group of people, such as users of flickr.com, attempts to do so, it can seem impossible. Many in the blogisphere have identified this as the primary reason for the popularity of free tagging and folksonomy, as in this post from Stewart Butterfield.

> I think the lack of hierarchy, synonym control and semantic precision are precisely why it works. Free typing loose associations is just a lot easier than making a decision about the degree of match to a pre-defined category (especially hierarchical ones). It's like 90% of the value of a "proper" taxonomy but 10 times simpler.[5]

In addition to simplifying vocabulary creation, social tagging and folksonomies are being used in novel ways to create communities. Connotea.com (see Figure 3.) is a free online reference management system for clinicians and scientists built around free tagging. Aside from its scientific focus, Connotea is distinguished from other social bookmarking sites by its emphasis on community building. In addition to displaying how many times a particular tag has been attached to a certain resource, Connotea also displays the usernames of the people using that tag. Registered users are also given the option of creating a "community page," essentially a wiki, around that tag. This leverages the folksonomy as an organic way to establish communities of practice across a wide range of interests. This in itself can be a strong incentive to invest some time and effort in tagging.

**Figure 3. Connotea communities can be built around tags.**

# Tag Clouds

Once someone gets into the tagging habit, it can become addictive. Just like the pictures on your home computer, tags can accumulate surprisingly quickly. This is especially true with public **tag spaces** in which multiple people add tags independent of each other. Without a simple way to visualize and navigate them, their value is lost. The **tag cloud** has emerged as the most popular approach.

A tag cloud is in essence a weighted list of terms. The visual emphasis given to each term in the list is a reflection of its popularity or frequency of use. For example, if a collection of tags centered on classical composers contained 10 instances of the tag "baroque," 50 of the tag "bach" and 300 of the tag "music" could be presented as:

baroque    bach    **music**

The size and weight of the font indicate the popularity of each of these tags in relation to the others. This example also demonstrates that tag displays are not directly proportionate to the number of its occurrences. If this were the case, obscure tags would be unreadably small while the most popular tags would take up the entire display. This is due to the fact that most tag collections follow a **power law**[6].

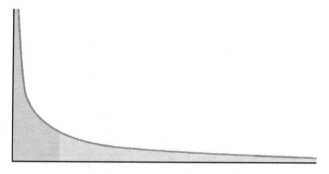

**Figure 4. A power law distribution curve.**

The idea of a power law was discussed in Chapter Four under the guise of the Pareto principle or the eighty-twenty rule. A power law is a long-tailed distribution curve in which a few items occur with very high frequency and most items occur with a very small frequency. As we saw with Flickr.com, a few tags such as **me**, **wedding**, **vacation** and the like, are used often by a lot of people. Most tags are more personal and idiosyncratic, occurring only a few times throughout the entire tag space. To reflect this, most tag displays use some form of proportional scaling so that common tags do not overwhelm more precise but less popular tags. A tag cloud will take all of the tags applied to a given collection, such as your

**Figure 5. A personal tag cloud from flickr.com.**

personal photos or bookmarks, apply the scaling factor, and present a picture of your collection and how you have organized it (see Figure 5). Beyond personal and individual collections, tag clouds often represent a public collection of information and the tags assigned to its resources by the community at large.

LibraryThing bills itself as a virtual, personal bookshelf that "also connects you with people who read the same things." The service lets you provide minimal information about a book you own or are reading and then provides professional, standard cataloging information. Library thing also lets you tag books in your collection and see how others have tagged the same title. This provides an interesting hybrid of professional and folk metadata. These tags are displayed as tag clouds giving a sense of how the central theme of a book, at least in the view of LibraryThing users. The cloud also affords a view into secondary themes and potentially novel associations. Users have tagged over twenty-five million books. These tags in are used for both findability and connecting users. Much like Connotea in the scientific community, LibraryThing attempts to build interest communities around tags and the books they describe.

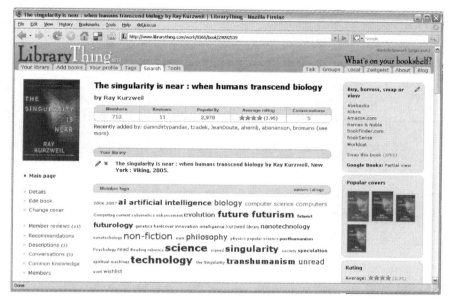

**Figure 6. LibraryThing organizes both personal and public tags.**

A tag cloud provides both a straight forward mechanism for visualizing an information space and a simple means to navigate it. Despite this and the current vogue of tag clouds, (they seem to be a mandatory component of any website with more than two pages of content) there is some debate over their usefulness. Thomas Vander Wal has referred to tag clouds as "the things that are cute but provide little value."[7] Designer Jeffrey Zeldman has publicly fretted about their reckless adoption. In his blog he writes:

> Like mood rings and fanny packs, like mullets and the
> Macarena, the weighted tag clouds meme popularized
> by Flickr and Technorati is about to cross a permanent
> cultural shame threshold. Brilliant as the idea remains,
> faddishness is choking its air supply. Damned clouds are
> everywhere.
>
> It's not just blogs that are using weighted tag clouds.
> Businesses   are   shoveling   them   into   interface
> makeovers, with predictably mixed success. Thus Lulu,
> a company that helps people publish their own books,
> CDs, and other products, offers a half-hearted tag
> cloud to help customers browse categories.
>
> It is of course wrong to compare weighted tag clouds to
> mullets, mood rings, and similar instances of mindless
> pop-cultural detritus. Tag clouds are not dumb. Their
> smartness is why so many have rushed to use them. But
> ubiquity and repetition quickly turn sweets to ashes.[8]

As implementers rush to jump on the free-tagging and tag cloud
bandwagon, they too often forget the fundamental issues that
taxonomies and controlled vocabularies are intended to solve.
Beyond the problems of synonymy, polysemy and the lack of
structured relationships between concepts, free-tagging in general and
tag clouds in particular raise specific issues which must be addressed.

The first issue is rooted in the way a tag cloud presents keywords and
how that display relates to the underlying collection of resources it
represents.  The power law inherent in tag collections is also the
Achilles heel of tag clouds.  Because there are no restrictions on
adding new keywords as tags, the sheer number of different tags in a
collection makes it impossible for a tag cloud to display more than a
few of the most popular.  The most popular tags also tend to be the
most general.  The emphasis on increasingly general tags is a self-
reinforcing phenomenon as noted by Scott Golder and Bernardo
Huberman of Hewlett-Packard's Information Dynamics Lab.

> As others have observed, some tags are used by many people, while other tags are used by fewer people. ... those tags that are generally meaningful will likely be used by many taggers, while tags with personal or specialized meaning will likely be used by fewer users. Users have a strong bias toward using general tags first.[9]

This is problematic in two ways. First, the keywords displayed in the tag cloud tend to be skewed toward popularity at the expense of findability. Relevant and potentially critical information will be pushed out of the display if a significant chunk of users do not find it interesting. This leads to the second problem, **occlusion**. When a tag cloud is the primary means of retrieval and access to a collection of information, if the tags associated with a particular resource are not popular enough to make the cut for the tag cloud, that resource is occluded. In other words, it is hidden and inaccessible. It may as well not be in the collection at all. James Sinclair and Michael Cardew-Hall of the Australian National University, found that this occlusion occurs for over half of the potentially relevant documents in information seeking sessions with a tag cloud. This has ramifications for the tag cloud as an information retrieval interface. According to Sinclair and Cardew-Hall:

> In every session of the experiment, a significant number of articles were not accessible from the tag cloud. Interestingly, while the number of tags in the cloud remained constant (70 tags), the number of occluded articles increased proportionally to the total number of articles. ... This inability to make all articles accessible from a single page is a major disadvantage compared with the search box. Hence, tag clouds are clearly not sufficient as the sole means of navigating a folksonomy dataset.[10]

Another, more intractable problem plagues folksonomies as a whole, regardless of how they are displayed and navigated. It is just too easy to create a tag. For many, this is the greatest strength of free-tagging, but in the long run it turns out to be its greatest weakness. As this entire book has demonstrated, creating useful metadata and taxonomies can be a difficult process requiring a great deal of thought and effort. Before a term is added to a taxonomy, the concept it describes must be understood in relation to the rest of the domain. The vocabulary of multiple audiences must be reconciled and the selected term vetted and adopted. With a folksonomy, a user can add a tag with almost no effort and even less thought. This low barrier to entry is a source of great consternation to Information Architects and what Clay Shirky calls the "well-designed metadata crowd."[11] Blogging about the issue, Louis Rosenfield writes:

> ...it's easy to say that the social networkers have figured out what the librarians haven't: a way to make metadata work in widely distributed and heretofore disconnected content collections. Easy, but wrong: folksonomies are clearly compelling; supporting a serendipitous form of browsing that can be quite useful. But they don't support searching and other types of browsing nearly as well as tags from controlled vocabularies applied by professionals. Folksonomies aren't likely to organically arrive at preferred terms for concepts, or even evolve synonymous clusters. They're highly unlikely to develop beyond flat lists and accrue the broader and narrower term relationships that we see in thesauri.[12]

These concerns are not just the fretting of stodgy librarians defending orthodoxy. When little thought goes into a tag or the tagger becomes more familiar with a subject, new and more appropriate tag terms are often discovered that better represent the concept or resource being tagged. This pattern was born out in the research of Hewlett Packard's Golder and Huberman.

> Users' tag lists grow over time, as they discover new interests and add new tags to categorize and describe them. Tags may exhibit very different growth rates, however, reflecting how users' interests develop and

> change over time. ... Because sensemaking is a
> retrospective process, information must be observed
> before one can establish its meaning. Therefore, a
> distinction may go unnoticed for a long time until it is
> finally created by the individual, who then continues to
> find that distinction important in making sense of
> future information. Since finding previously
> encountered information is extremely important, this is
> deeply problematic for past information.[13]

As tags accumulate over time and the breadth and depth of the
tagged content grows, it becomes all but impossible to retroactively
add newer and more precise terms to previously tagged content.
Over time, older tags become overwhelmed by newer tags and the
earlier tagged resources become occluded and lost. Despite these
difficulties, free-tagging and folksonomies have passionate
champions who make often compelling cases. Clay Shirky sums up
the argument nicely in his social software blog "Many 2 Many."

> The advantage of folksonomies isn't that they're better
> than controlled vocabularies, it's that they're better
> than nothing, because controlled vocabularies are not
> extensible to the majority of cases where tagging is
> needed. Building, maintaining, and enforcing a
> controlled vocabulary is, relative to folksonomies,
> enormously expensive, both in the development time,
> and in the cost to the user, especially the amateur
> user, in using the system.[14]

So we are left with a quandary. If we adopt a free-tagging,
folksonomic approach we run a risk of drowning in misleading
metadata and buried information. If we reject folksonomies
altogether, we are likely to end up with no metadata at all. So what
are we to do? The solution, of course, is to find a middle ground.

# *Pace Layering*

In the book *How Buildings Learn*, Whole Earth Catalog founder Stewart Brand proposes that buildings and societies are comprised of several layers that each grow or evolve at their own rate (see Figure 7).[15]    Consider a house.    You may change the pictures and decorations on the walls every few weeks as the whim strikes you. Painting those walls takes a bit more effort and so may only be done every year or so.    Putting in a new carpet or wood floor might happen every five years.  Adding a room is a very rare occurrence and the foundation of the house itself will probably not change throughout the life of the home.

This notion of varying levels of stability and volatility is as relevant to websites and information spaces as it is to cities and brick-and-mortar buildings.    In any complex system, the fast layers propose and innovate; the slow layers absorb and stabilize.[16]   The Information Architecture of a website and the core metadata supporting search are worth considerable investment in time and resources.  Semantic integration, system scalability, targeted promotion and relationship continuity all require planning and stability.  Blogs, reviews, ratings and consumer content require flexibility and responsiveness.

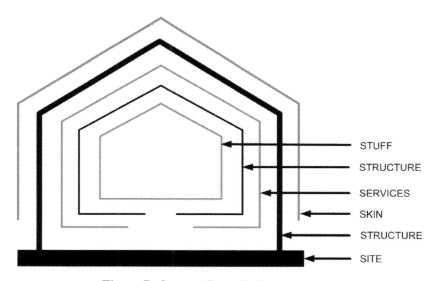

STUFF

STRUCTURE

SERVICES

SKIN

STRUCTURE

SITE

**Figure 7.  Stewart Brand's Pace Layering**

| | Architectural Components | The Iceberg of IA | Elements of User Experience | Planes of User Experience |
|---|---|---|---|---|
| **Fast** ↑ | Content, services, interface | Interface | Visual Design | Surface |
| | Adaptive finding tools | Wireframes Blueprints | Interface design Navigation design Information design | Skeleton |
| | Controlled vocabulary | Metadata Classification schemes Thesauri | Interaction design Information architecture | Structure |
| | Enabling technologies | IA strategies Project plans | Functional specifications Content requirements | Scope |
| | Embedded navigation system | Users (needs, behaviors) Content (structure, meaning) Context (culture, technology) | User needs Site objectives | Strategy |
| **Slow** | Faceted classification schemes | | | |

**Figure 8. Pace layering as applied to Information Architecture.**

Designers and Information architects have acknowledged this and are adopting the pace layering world view (see Figure 8).[17]

This view reconciles the rigid world of formal metadata and taxonomy with the anarchy of free-tagging and folksonomy. Peter Morville sums up this view nicely in his book Ambient Findability:

> But that's the beauty of the boundary object we call metadata. We don't have to choose. Ontologies, taxonomies, and folksonomies are not mutually exclusive. In many contexts, such as corporate web sites, the formal structure of ontologies and taxonomies is worth the investment. In others, like the blogosphere, the casual serendipity of folksonomies is certainly better than nothing. And in some contexts, such as intranets and knowledge networks, a hybrid metadata ecology that combines elements of each may be ideal.[19]

As noted in previous chapters, a taxonomy is never finished. Once deployed it must be maintained with constant revision and refinement if it is to stay relevant. Free-tagging and folksonomy is one way to stay in touch with users and to monitor how terminology evolves over time.    Site like Amazon.com are beginning to incorporate this into their content strategies, assigning books and DVDs slots in their product hierarchies with corporate assigned keywords, but also allowing customers to assign and share keywords that they find relevant.  Those tags that become common may find their way into the official taxonomy.  This type of "Bubble-up classification" can keep a taxonomy and the applications it supports vibrant and useful.

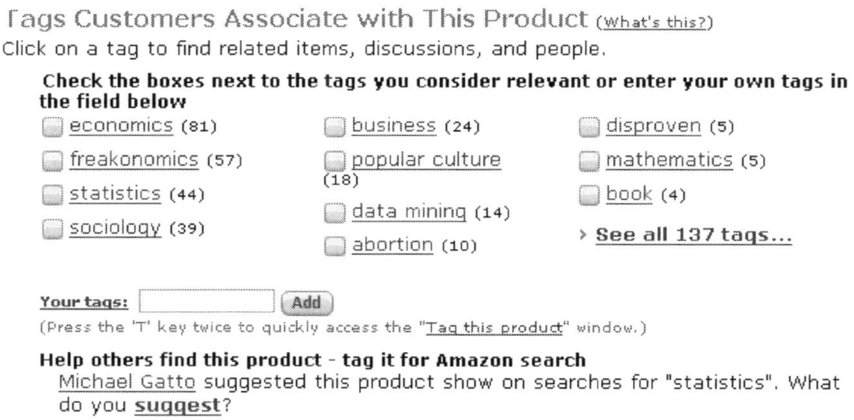

Tags Customers Associate with This Product (What's this?)
Click on a tag to find related items, discussions, and people.

Check the boxes next to the tags you consider relevant or enter your own tags in the field below
◻ economics (81)          ◻ business (24)          ◻ disproven (5)
◻ freakonomics (57)       ◻ popular culture         ◻ mathematics (5)
◻ statistics (44)           (18)
                          ◻ data mining (14)        ◻ book (4)
◻ sociology (39)
                          ◻ abortion (10)           › **See all 137 tags...**

**Your tags:** [                ] ( Add )
(Press the 'T' key twice to quickly access the "Tag this product" window.)

**Help others find this product - tag it for Amazon search**
  Michael Gatto suggested this product show on searches for "statistics". What do you suggest?

**Figure 9.    Consumer tags supplementing formal classification at Amazon.com.**

Acknowledging and managing this dynamic is critical to the ongoing success of any information ecosystem.  There is a dangerous flip-side to the enlivening aspects Brand's pace layering.  In explaining the dynamics between the different layers of a structure he said, "because of the different rates of change of its components, a building is always tearing itself apart"[20]  Our information environments will change and evolve despite our best efforts to maintain the structure we have labored so long and hard to create.  Rather than guardians of stability we should become shepherds of evolution, watching for insight and innovation, discarding the chaff while preserving, incorporating and promoting the useful.

# Glossary

The definitions in this glossary are drawn from ANSI/NISO Z39.19 – 2005. They are not a part of the formal standard but are included as representing a general consensus of related standards, specialized dictionaries, and industry experts. The full standard, including this glossary, is available online at

www.niso.org/standards/resources/Z39-19.html

**associative relationship** A relationship between or among terms in a controlled vocabulary that leads from one term to other terms that are related to or associated with it; begins with the words SEE ALSO or related term (RT).

**asymmetric** Lacking symmetry. In the context of controlled vocabularies, reciprocal relationships are asymmetric when the relationship indicator used between a pair of linked terms is different in one direction than it is in the reverse direction, e.g. BT / NT.

**authority file** A set of established headings and the cross-references to be made to and from each heading, often citing the authority for the preferred form or variants. Types of authority files include name authority files and subject authority files.

**blind reference** 1. A term in a controlled vocabulary that has not been assigned to any content objects. These may be needed in some instances as place holders in taxonomies and other structured vocabularies. 2. A preferred term used in a SEE or USE reference where the term pointed to does not exist in the vocabulary

**bound term** A term consisting of a compound term or phrase that indicates a single concept. See also *compound term.*

**bound term** A term consisting of a compound term or phrase that indicates a single concept. See also *compound term*.

**broader term** A term to which another term or multiple terms are subordinate in a hierarchy. In thesauri, the relationship indicator for this type of term is BT.

**candidate term** A term under consideration for admission into a controlled vocabulary because of its potential usefulness. Also known as *provisional term*.

**category** A grouping of terms that are semantically or statistically associated, but which do not constitute a strict hierarchy based on genus/species, parent/child, or part/whole relationships. See also *tree structure*.

**classification scheme** A method of organization according to a set of pre-established principles, usually characterized by a notation system and a hierarchical structure of relationships among the entities.

**compound term** A term consisting of more than one word or a phrase that represents a single concept. Compound terms **must** be constructed according to the guidelines of this Standard.
See also *bound term* and *precoordination*.

**concept** A unit of thought, formed by mentally combining some or all of the characteristics of a concrete or abstract, real or imaginary object. Concepts exist in the mind as abstract entities independent of terms used to express them.
**concept map** A representation in two dimensions of the conceptual relationships among terms and the concepts they represent.

**content object** An entity that contains data/information. A content object can itself be made up of content objects. For example, a journal is a content object made up of individual journal articles, which can each be a content object. The text, figures, and photographs included in a journal article can also be separate content objects. Paintings, sculpture, maps, photographs, and other non-textual objects are also content objects. The metadata for a content object can itself be a content object.

**controlled vocabulary** A list of terms that have been enumerated explicitly. This list is controlled by and is available from a controlled vocabulary registration authority. All terms in a controlled vocabulary *must* have an unambiguous, non-redundant definition.

**cross-reference** A direction from one term to another. See *associative relationship*; *equivalence relationship*; *hierarchical relationship*.

**descriptor** See *preferred term*.

**difference** See *modifier*.

**entry term** The non-preferred term in a cross reference that leads to a term in a controlled vocabulary. Also known as "lead-in term." In thesauri, the relationship indicator for this type of term is U (USE); its reciprocal is UF (USED FOR). See also *preferred term*.

**entry vocabulary** The set of non-preferred terms (USE references) that lead to terms in a controlled vocabulary.

**eponym** A term incorporating the name of a real or mythical person, generally the discoverer of a phenomenon or inventor of an object, e.g., Herculean labor, Parkinson's disease, pasteurization.

**equivalence relationship** A relationship between or among terms in a controlled vocabulary that leads to one or more terms that are to be used instead of the term from which the cross-reference is made; begins with the word
SEE or USE.

**facet** A grouping of concepts of the same inherent category. Examples of categories that may be used for grouping concepts into facets are: activities, disciplines, people, materials, places, etc.

**facet indicator** See *node label.*

**federated searching** See *metasearching.*

**filing rules** A set of guidelines that determine how letters and numbers, spaces, and special characters will be treated in assembling an alphabetical or other listing.

**flat format** An alphabetical display format of controlled vocabularies in which only one level of broader terms and one level of narrower terms are shown for each term.

**focus** In a compound term, the noun component that identifies the class of concepts to which the term as a whole refers. Also known as *head noun.* See also *modifier.*

**free text** Antonym of controlled vocabulary. Natural language terms appearing in content objects, which can complement controlled vocabulary terms in an information storage and retrieval system. In free text searching, controlled vocabulary terms can also be retrieved. See also *keyword.*

**generic posting** 1. In controlled vocabularies, the treatment of narrower terms as equivalents, e.g., **furniture** UF beds; UF sofas. See also *upposting.* 2. In indexing and subject cataloging, the assignment of a broader term instead of a specific term, e.g., **furniture** to a content object on sofas.

**generic structure** A controlled vocabulary format that indicates all hierarchical levels of terms within an alphabetic display by means of codes, indentation, and/or punctuation marks.

**gloss** An explanation or definition of an obscure or ambiguous word in a text. See also *qualifier.*

**heading** A preferred name or term. Types of headings include proper name headings (which may be called identifiers), subject headings, and terms. A heading may include a *qualifier.*

**hierarchical relationship** . A relationship between or among terms in a controlled vocabulary that depicts broader (generic) to narrower (specific) or whole-part relationships; begins with the words broader term (BT), or narrower term (NT).

**hierarchy** Broader (generic) to narrower (specific) or whole-part relationships, which are generally indicated in a controlled vocabulary through codes or indentation. See also *broader term; narrower term.*

**history note** A note in a term record in a controlled vocabulary that provides the date of entry of a term as well as the history of modifications to its scope, relationships, etc.

**homograph** One of two or more words that have the same spelling, but different meanings and origins. In controlled vocabularies, homographs are generally distinguished by *qualifiers.*

**identifier** 1. A proper name (or its abbreviation or acronym) of an institution, person, place, object, or process, optionally treated as a category of heading distinct from terms. Identifiers may be held in a separate file (compare authority file), and their form may be controlled (e.g., the name of an international organization having different names in various languages, only one of which is selected).
2. In some systems, a provisional term that may be upgraded to approved status, or a highly specific term that is not eligible for term status, but which is considered useful for retrieval and is assigned to one or more content objects without vocabulary control.

**indexing** 1. A method by which terms or subject headings from a controlled vocabulary are selected by a human or computer to represent the concepts in or attributes of a content object. The terms may or may not occur in the content object. 2. An operation intended to represent the results of the content analysis of a document by means of a controlled indexing language or by natural language. [ISO 5127/1]

**indexing language** A controlled vocabulary or classification system and the rules for its application. An indexing language is used for the representation of concepts dealt with in documents [content objects] and for the retrieval of such documents [content objects] from an information storage and retrieval system. [ISO 5127/1]

**indexing term** The representation of a concept in an indexing language, generally in the form of a noun or noun phrase. Terms, subject headings, and heading-subheading combinations are examples of indexing terms.

**interoperability** The ability of two or more systems or components to exchange information and use the exchanged information without special effort on the part of either system.

**keyword** A word occurring in the natural language of a document that is considered significant for indexing and retrieval. See also *free text*.

**KWIC (Key Word In Context) index.** A type of index, arranged alphabetically, in which each significant word in a string of text serves as an access point, by being graphically emphasized and surrounded by the rest of the string. The keyword is generally in a centered column and is followed on the right by the continuation of the string, which provides the context. The balance of the string, if any, is positioned to the left of the keyword.

**KWOC (Key Word Out Of Context) index** A type of index, arranged alphabetically, in which each significant word in a string of text serves as an access point, usually positioned in the left-hand column of a page, followed by the complete string. The keyword may therefore not be in the immediate context of the words that surround it.

**lexeme** A fundamental unit of the vocabulary of a language.

**lexical database** A database containing terms as well as information about the terms such as part of speech, type of term, etc.

**lexicographer** A person who is knowledgeable about terms, their uses, parts of speech, etc. Lexicographers often construct controlled vocabularies.

**literary warrant** Justification for the representation of a concept in an indexing language or for the selection of a preferred term because of its frequent occurrence in the literature. See also *organizational warrant* and *user warrant*.

**mapping** A set of correspondences between categories, schema element names, or controlled terms. Mappings are used for transforming data or queries from one vocabulary for use with another.

**metasearching** The simultaneous searching across multiple databases, sources, platforms, and protocols. Also known as broadcast searching, cross-database searching, federated searching, or parallel searching.

**modifier** In a compound term, one or more components that serve to narrow the extension of a focus and specify one of its subclasses. Also known as *difference*.

**multilevel hierarchy** A set of hierarchical relationships among terms that has multiple levels of specificity extending from the most broadly defined terms to the most specific.

**narrower term** A term that is subordinate to another term or to multiple terms in a hierarchy. In thesauri, the relationship indicator for this type of term is NT.

**natural language** A language used by human beings for verbal communication. Words extracted from natural language texts for indexing purposes without vocabulary control are often called keywords.

**navigation** The process of moving through a controlled vocabulary or an information space via some pre-established links or relationships. For example, navigation in a controlled vocabulary could mean moving from a broader term to one or more narrower terms using the predefined relationships.

**near-synonym** A term whose meaning is not exactly synonymous with that of another term, yet which may nevertheless be treated as its equivalent in a controlled vocabulary. Example: **salinity, saltiness**

**node label** A "dummy" term, often a phrase, that is not assigned to documents when indexing, but which is inserted into the hierarchical section of some controlled vocabularies to indicate the logical basis on which a class has been divided. Node labels may also be used to group categories of related terms in the alphabetic section of a controlled vocabulary.

**non-preferred term** See *entry term*. See also *preferred term*.

**organizational warrant** Justification for the representation of a concept in an indexing language or for the selection of a preferred term due to characteristics and context of the organization. See also *literary warrant* and *user warrant*.

**orphan term** A term that has no associative or hierarchical relationship to any other term in a controlled vocabulary.

**orthography** The art of writing words with the proper letters according to standard usage.

**permuted display** A type of index where individual words of a term are rotated to bring each word of the term into alphabetical order in the term list. See also *KWIC* and *KWOC*.

**polyhierarchy** A controlled vocabulary structure in which some terms belong to more than one hierarchy. For example, **rose** might be a narrower term under both **flowers** and **perennials** in a horticulture vocabulary.

**polyseme** A word with multiple meanings. In spoken language, polysemes are called homonyms; in written language they are called homographs. Only the latter are relevant to controlled vocabularies designed for textual information.

**postcoordination** The combining of terms at the searching stage rather than at the subject heading list construction stage or indexing stage. See also *precoordination*.

**postings** The number of content objects to which a term is assigned.

**precision** A measure of a search system's ability to retrieve only relevant content objects. Usually expressed as a percentage calculated by dividing the number of retrieved relevant content objects by the total number of content objects retrieved. A high-precision search ensures that, for the most part, the content objects retrieved will be relevant. However, a high-precision search may not retrieve all relevant content objects. See also *recall*. Recall and precision tend to be inverse ratios. When one goes up, the other usually goes down.

**precoordination** The formulation of a multiword heading or the linking of a heading and subheadings to create a formally controlled, multi-element expression of a concept or object. Precoordination is often used to ensure logical sorting of related expressions. Examples of precoordinated headings:

> **New England—Genealogy—Handbooks, Manuals, etc.**
> **Searching, Bibliographic**
> **United States—History—Civil War, 1861-1865**

See also *postcoordination*.

**preferred term** One of two or more synonyms or lexical variants selected as a term for inclusion in a controlled vocabulary. See also *non-preferred term*.

**provisional term** See *candidate term*.

**qualifier** A defining term, used in a controlled vocabulary to distinguish homographs. A qualifier is considered part of a term, subject heading, or entry term, but is separated from it by punctuation. The qualifier is generally enclosed in parentheses. Example: **Mercury (metal)**
See also *gloss*.

**quasi-synonym** See *near synonym*.

**recall** A measure of a search system's ability to retrieve all relevant content objects. Usually expressed as a percentage calculated by dividing the number of retrieved relevant content objects by the number of all relevant content objects in a collection. A high recall search retrieves a comprehensive set of relevant content objects from the collection. However, high recall increases the possibility that less relevant content objects will also be retrieved. See also *precision*. Recall and precision tend to be inverse ratios. When one goes up, the other usually goes down.

**reciprocity** Semantic relationships in controlled vocabularies must be reciprocal, that is each relationship from one term to another must also be represented by a reciprocal relationship in the other direction. Reciprocal relationships may be symmetric, e.g. RT / RT, or asymmetric e.g. BT / NT. See also *asymmetric* and *symmetric*.

**related term** A term that is associatively but not hierarchically linked to another term in a controlled vocabulary. In thesauri, the relationship indicator for this type of term is RT.

**relationship indicator** A word, phrase, abbreviation, or symbol used in thesauri to identify a semantic relationship between terms.

Examples of relationship indicators are UF (USED FOR), and RT (related term).

**scope note** A note following a term explaining its coverage, specialized usage, or rules for assigning it.

**semantic linking** A method of linking terms according to their meaning or meanings.

**semantic web** A representation in two (or possibly three) dimensions of the semantic relationships between and among terms and the concepts they represent.

**sibling** A term that shares the same broader term (one level higher) as other terms.

**stop list** A list of words considered to be of no value for retrieval. It consists primarily of function words—articles, conjunctions, and prepositions— but may also include words that occur very frequently in the literature of a domain.

**subheading** A term appended to a heading in order to modify or delimit the heading by indicating a particular aspect or relationship pertaining to it. A term with a subheading may be subject to further modification. See also *precoordination*.

**subject heading** A word or phrase, or any combination of words, phrases, and modifiers used to describe the topic of a content object. Precoordination of terms for multiple and related concepts is a characteristic of subject headings that distinguishes them from controlled vocabulary terms. See also *precoordinated term* and *precoordination*.

**subject heading list** An alphabetical list of subject headings with cross references from non-preferred terms and links to related terms. These lists often include separate sequences of standardized subheadings that may be combined with all or only some subject headings. Rules for applying subheadings usually accompany such lists.

**symmetric** Having symmetry. In the context of controlled vocabularies reciprocal relationships are symmetric when the relationship indicator used between a pair of linked terms is the same in one direction as it is in the reverse direction, e.g. RT / RT. See also *asymmetric* and *reciprocity*.

**synonym** A word or term having exactly or very nearly the same meaning as another word or term.

**synonym ring** A group of terms that are considered equivalent for the purposes of retrieval.

**taxonomy** A collection of controlled vocabulary terms organized into a hierarchical structure. Each term in a taxonomy is in one or more parent/child (broader/narrower) relationships to other terms in the taxonomy.

**term** One or more words designating a concept. See also *compound term, entry term*, and *precoordinated term*.

**term record** A collection of information associated with a term in a controlled vocabulary, including the history of the term, its relationships to other terms, and, optionally, authorities for the term.

**thesaurus**
A controlled vocabulary arranged in a known order and structured so that the various relationships among terms are displayed clearly and identified by standardized relationship indicators. Relationship indicators ***should*** be employed reciprocally. Its purpose is to promote consistency in the indexing of content objects, especially for postcoordinated information storage and retrieval systems, and to facilitate browsing and searching by linking entry terms with terms. Thesauri may also facilitate the retrieval of content objects in free text searching.

**top term** The broadest term in a controlled vocabulary hierarchy, sometimes indicated by the abbreviation TT.

**tree structure** A controlled vocabulary display format in which the complete hierarchy of terms is shown. Each term is assigned a tree number or line number which leads from the alphabetical display to the hierarchical one. The hierarchical display is also known as a *systematic display*.

**user warrant** Justification for the representation of a concept in an indexing language or for the selection of a preferred term because of frequent requests for information on the concept or free-text searches on the term by users of an information storage and retrieval system. See also *literary warrant* and *organizational warrant*.

**vocabulary control** The process of organizing a list of terms (a) to indicate which of two or more synonymous terms is authorized for use; (b) to distinguish between homographs; and (c) to indicate hierarchical and associative relationships among terms in the context of a controlled vocabulary or subject heading list. See also *controlled vocabulary*.

# Notes

## CHAPTER ONE: FINDABILITY

1. Robert Blumberg and Atre Shaku. "The Problem with Unstructured Data." DM Review. February 2003: 42-46.
2. Alison J. Head. "Why Research Intranets Fail." Scrip.Online. March 25, 2003: 1-4.
3. Diagnostic Strategies "Benchmarking in Call Centers." 2001 whitepaper: 7.
4. Regina Casonato and Kathy Harris. "The Knowledge Worker Investment Paradox." July 17, 2002. Gartner Research. Report SPA-17-2363.
5. Susan Feldman and Chris Sherman, "The High Cost of Not Finding Information." IDC, June 2003. Whitepaper: 4.
6. Kit Sims-Taylor, "The Brief Reign of the Knowledge Worker." http://distance.ed.bcc.ctc.edu/econ/kst/BriefReign/BRwebversion.html.
7. Feldman and Sherman, 8.
8. Peter Lyman and Hal R. Varian, "How Much Information," 2003. http://www.sims.berkeley.edu/how-much-info-2003.
9. Blumberg and Shaku, 45.
10. Amanda Spink, et al. "From E-Sex to E-Commerce: Web Search Changes." Computer, 35(3). March 2002, 107-109.
11. Sergey Brin and Lawrence Page. "The Anatomy of a Large-Scale Hypertextual Web Search Engine." Computer Networks and ISDN Systems. 30 (1–7), April 1998. 107–117.
12. http://www.google.com/faq_freewebsearch.html.
13. It is important to note that this is not the case with Google's commercial solutions the Search Appliance and Google Mini. These tools are designed for enterprise search and can function quite well. They are, however, not free. Currently the Google

Search Appliance starts at $30,000 and the Google Mini at $2,995.

14. Feldman and Sherman, 8.

15. M. A. Katz, and M. D. Byrne. "Effects of Scent and Breadth on Use of Site-specific Search on E-Commerce Web Sites." ACM Transactions on Computer-Human Interaction. 10(3): 198-220.

16. Jaime Teevan, et al. "The perfect search engine is not enough: a study of orienteering behavior in directed search." In CHI '04: Proc. of the SIGCHI conf. on Human factors in computing systems: 415—422.

17. Google Whacking attempts to formulate a query with a single match.

18. Christine Alvarado, et al. "Surviving the information explosion: how people find their electronic information." Technical report MIT, April 2003.

19. K. Straub, and A. Valdes. "The Search is Over: The Answer is Browse." Cited in K Schaffer,. UI Design Newsletter, January 2005. http://www.humanfactors.com/downloads/jan05.asp#kath

20. Peter Pirolli and Stuart Card. "Information foraging in information access environments." Proceedings of the Conference on Human Factors in Computing Systems (CHI'95): 51–58.

21. Rachel Chalmers. "Surf like a Bushman." New Scientist. 11 November 2000: 93-41.

22. Jakob Nielson. "Deceivingly Strong Information Scent Costs Sales." Alert Box, 2 August 2004, http://www.useit.com/alertbox/20040802.html.

23. Delphi Group. "Taxonomy & Content Classification Market." Milestone Report, 2002: 22.

## CHAPTER TWO: METADATA

1. The answer is Vannevar Bush, who wrote the seminal "As We May Think." The Atlantic Monthly, July 1945.

2. Arlene G. Taylor, The Organization of Information. Second Edition (Westport, CT: Libraries Unlimited, 2004), 147-148.

3. Darin Stewart, "Flow Control." Intelligent Enterprise, 21 February 2002, 43.
4. Sherry L Vellucci. "Metadata and Authority Control." Library Resources and Technical Services 44(1): 33–43.
5. Christine L Borgman. "From Acting Locally to Thinking Globally: A Brief History of Library Automation." Library Quarterly. 67:2,1 1997, 5-49.
6. Thomas Baker. "A Grammar of Dublin Core." D-Lib Magazine. 6 (10), October 2000.
7. National Information Standards Organization. "Understanding Metadata." NISO 2004.
8. Taylor, 153.
9. Dublin Core Metadata Initiative (DCMI) recommendation 6/13/2006.

## CHAPTER THREE: TAXONOMY

1. George Lakoff. "Women, Fire and Dangerous Things." (University of Chicago Press. 1990), 5.
2. Wikipedia entry for Intertwingularity. Retrieved 29 August 2006, http://en.wikipedia.org/wiki/Intertwingularity.

3. Ted Nelson. "Computer Lib/Dream Machines. Revised & Updated." Microsoft Press. 1987.
4. Aristotle's student Theophrastus (ca. 370 to 285 BCE) named and classified 480 species of plant and is often called the "Father of Botany." A century and a half later Dioscorides, a Greek physician in the Roman Army. published Materia Medica, which classified 600 kinds of plants according to their medicinal qualities.
5. Gary L. Bunker and Davis Bitton. "The Mormon Graphic Image 1834-1914: Cartoons, Caricatures, and Illustrations." Salt Lake City: U of U Press, 1983.
6. Adapted from Maewyn Cumming "Tomatoes are not the only fruit." UKgovTalk, 29 April 2005. http://www.govtalk.gov.uk/schemasstandard/gcl_document.asp?docnum=681.

7.  These relationships are codified in the formal ISO standard 2788:1986: "Documentation—Guidelines for the establishment and development of monolingual thesauri."

8.  Jan Wyllie. Taxonomies: Frameworks for Corporate Knowledge, Second Edition, (London, England: Ark Group, 2006), 128.

9.  Sayers, W. C. B. A Manual of Classification for Librarians, Fourth Edition. (London, England: Andre Deutsch 1967), 32.

10. S. R. Ranganathan, "Philosophy of Library Classification." Copenhagen: E. Munksgaard. 1951, 32.

11. Taylor, 302.

12. Barbara H. Kwasnick. "The role of classification in knowledge representation and discovery." Library Trends 48 (1): 22-47.

## CHAPTER FOUR: PREPARATIONS

1.  See Robert T. Clemen's Making Hard Decisions, Second Edition (Belmont, California: Duxbury Press, 1996). An introduction to Decision Analysis" for an outstanding introduction to getting reasonable estimates from stakeholders.

## CHAPTER FIVE: TERMS

1.  Susan Awe. "ARBA Guide to Subject Encyclopedias and Dictionaries. Second Edition." (Libraries Unlimited, 1997).

2.  www.getty.edu/research/conducting_research/vocabularies/tgn/

3.  authorities.loc.gov.

## CHAPTER SIX: STRUCTURE

1.  Lou Rosenfeld and Peter Morville. Information Architecture for the World Wide Web, second edition. (Cambridge, England: O'Rielly Media.), 235.

2.  Louise Spiteri. "A Simplified Model for Facet Analysis." Canadian Journal of Information and Library Science v23, 1-30 (April-July 1998).

3. V. Broughton, "Faceted classification as a basis for knowledge organization in a digital environment; the Bliss Bibliographic Classification as a model for vocabulary management and the creation of multi-dimensional knowledge structures." The New Review of Hypermedia and Multimedia 2001: 67-102.

## CHAPTER SEVEN: INTEROPERABILITY

1. It is important to note that in order to take advantage of namespaces, an XML schema must be created rather than a DTD.
2. http://zthes.z3950.org/schema/index.html

## CHAPTER EIGHT: ONTOLOGY

1. Punam Bedi, Sudeep Marwaha, Designing Ontologies from Traditional Taxonomies, Proc. ICCS'04 - International Conference on Cognitive Science, Allahabad, India, December 16-18, 2004, 324 – 329.
2. Natalya F. Noy, Deborah L. McGuinness. "Ontology Development 101: A Guide to Creating Your First Ontology."http://protege.stanford.edu/publications/ontology_development/ontology101-noy-mcguinness.html
3. Li Ding, et al., "Using Ontologies in the Semantic Web: A Survey" [Electronic Version]. July 20, 2005. Retrieved January 2, 2008 from http://ebiquity.umbc.edu/paper/html/id/266/Using-Ontologies-in-the-Semantic-Web-A-Survey
4. Natalya F. Noy and Deborah L. McGuinness. ``Ontology Development 101: A Guide to Creating Your First Ontology''. Stanford Knowledge Systems Laboratory Technical Report KSL-01-05 and Stanford Medical Informatics Technical Report SMI-2001-0880, March 2001.
5. Passin, 47
6. W3C. OWL Web Ontology Language Overview W3C Recommendation 10 February 2004. Retrieved on January 2, 2008. http://www.w3.org/TR/owl-features/
7. Grigoris Antoniou and Frank van Harmelen. A Semantic Web Primer. (Cambridge, Massachusetts: The MIT Press. 2004), 111.

8. W3C.    OWL  Web  Ontology  Language  Overview.    W3C
   Recommendation           10           February           2004.
   http://www.w3.org/TR/owl-features/

## CHAPTER NINE: FOLKSONOMY

1. Golder, Scott A. & Huberman, Bernardo A. "The Structure of
   Collaborative     Tagging     Systems."     Hewlett-Packard     Labs,
   Information Dynamics Lab.
   http://arxiv.org/ftp/cs/papers/0508/0508082.pdf.
2. Star, Susan Leigh. 1996. "Slouching toward Infrastructure."
   Digital Libraries Conference Workshop. Illinois Research Group
   on Classification. Graduate School of Library and Information
   Science University of Illinois. Accessed June 15, 2007.
3. Thomas Vander Wal. "Folksonomy Coinage and Definition."
   February 2, 2007. www.vanderwal.net/folksonomy.html.
4. David Sifry.  "Technorati Launches Tags."  January 17, 2005.
   http://www.sifry.com/alerts/archives/000270.html.
5. Stewart     Butterfield.     personal     blog.     August     4,     2004.
   http://www.sylloge.com/personal/2004/08/folksonomy-social-
   classification- great.html.
6. Gene Smith. Tagging: People-Powered Metadata for the Social
   Web. (Berkeley, California: New Riders Press, 2008), 53.
7. Vander Wal, Thomas.
            www.vanderwal.net/random/category.php?cat=153
8. Jeffery Zeldman. "Tag Clouds are the New Mullets."  19 April
   2005. www.zeldman.com/daily/0405d.shtml.
9. Scott Golder and Bernardo A. Huberman. "Usage Patterns of
   Collaborative Tagging Systems." Journal of Information Science,
   32(2), 2006, 198-208.
10. James Sinclair and Michael Cardew- Hall. "The folksonomy tag
    cloud: when is it useful?" February 1, 2008. Journal of
    Information Science, Vol. 34, No. 1, 15-29.
11. Shirky, Clay.  Folksonomies + Controlled Vocabularies. January
    7, 2005.

12. http://many.corante.com/archives/2005/01/07/folksonomies_c ontrolled_vocabularies.php
13. Rosenfeld, Louis. "Folksonomies? How about Metadata Ecologies?" January 6, 2005. louisrosenfeld.com/home/bloug_archive/000330.html
14. Golder and Huberman. 2006, 198-208.
15. Shirky, Clay. Folksonomies + Controlled Vocabularies. January 7, 2005. http://many.corante.com/archives/2005/01/07/folksonomies_c ontrolled_vocabularies.php.
16. Stewart Brand. How Buildings Learn: What Happens After they're Built. (New York, New York: Penguin, 1994), 13.
17. Stewart Brand. The Clock of the Long Now: Time and Responsibility. (New York, New York: Basic Books), 45.
18. Campbell, D. Grant and Karl V. Fast. "From Pace Layering to Resilience Theory: The Complex Implications of Tagging for Information Architecture." IA Summit, 25 March 2006.
19. Peter Morville. Ambient Findability. (Cambridge, England: O'Rielly Media: 2007), 139.
20. Brand. 1994, 13.

# Index

## Z